Element(ary)
My Dear

Edited by: A.J. Huffman

and April Salzano

Cover Art: "Elements" collage by A.J. Huffman & Nancy Larsen

Copyright © 2015 A.J. Huffman

All rights reserved. Except for brief quotations in critical articles or reviews, no part of this book may be reproduced in any manner without prior written permission from the publisher:

Kind of a Hurricane Press
www.kindofahurricanepress.com
kindofahurricanepress@yahoo.com

CONTENTS

Featured Piece

Emily Strauss	*Personal Geology*	13

From the Authors

Sandra Anfang	*Silicon*	17
Carol Alena Aronoff	*Blood of the Soil*	18
	In a Time of Drought	19
Allen Ashley	*Across the Ether*	20
Harvey J. Baine	*Bee Lake*	23
Barbara Bald	*The Grudge*	24
James Bell	*The Wind Notices the Season*	25
Lana Bella	*The Bent Air*	26
	The Dry Bone	27
Nancy Boutilier	*Emily Dreaming*	28
Therese Broderick	*The Uncle Whose Only Daughter Died*	29
Tanya Bryan	*Holy Fire Painting with Yves Klein*	31
Jane Burn	*Harpyiai*	32
Janet Rice Carnahan	*Joining Forces*	33
	United Purpose	34
Alan Catlin	*The Elements*	35

Alexis Child	Alchemical Wedding	37
Joan Colby	Fire	38
	Electrical Fire	39
Esteban Colon	The Secret Life of Fire	40
Craig Cornish	Mountain Storm	41
	Just Fishing	43
Chella Courington	Shrouded in Mist	44
	Late Harvest	45
Susan Dale	Down the Pacific Coast	46
	Of Earth	49
Chip Dameron	Tibetan Prayer Flags	50
Theresa Darling	Days Without Anger – Day 7	51
Brindley Hallam Dennis	After the Deluge	52
Evelyn Deshane	Four Elements of Woman	54
Eric Dodson	Slow Motion	56
Karen Douglass	Eating Local	57
morgan downie	Urgedanke	58
Inna Dulchevsky	Transcendence	60
J.K. Durick	Small Star Poem	61
	Fire	62
Lucia Galloway	Dinner After the Storm	64

Brigitte Goetze	After the Eruption	65
Joan Goodreau	Northern Woman	66
Rick Hartwell	Flight Plan	67
H. Edgar Hix	Storm	68
Ruth Holzer	Mitigation	69
	Breathing	70
Liz Hufford	In the Japanese Garden	71
W. Luther Jett	The Elements	72
	Golem	73
Michael Lee Johnson	Moon Sleep	74
	Lost in the Distant Harbor	75
Lori Kiefer	Returning	76
	Sky Note	77
Noel King	Danger	78
Steve Klepetar	To the River of Flame	79
	Balm in the Wind	80
	Sailboats on the Beach	81
Andrea Lewis	Strike Anywhere	82
Lyn Lifshin	Fire	85
Jack e Lorts	Ephram Pratt Remembers Time in the Garden	87
	Ephram Pratt Sings to the Sun	88

Hillary Lyon	Aphrodite Rides the Bus	90
	Fleurs de Feu	91
	To a Drill Bit, Now a Bookend	92
Jennifer MacBain-Stephens	The Stuntwoman Considers Ending It All	93
	Solstice	95
Don Mager	January Journal: Saturday, January 26, 2013	97
	October Journal: Friday, October 18, 2013	98
Susan Mahan	Smoldering	99
Kim Malinowski	Water	100
	Air	101
Amanda M. May	Elements of Evaluation	102
Joan McNerney	East River, New York City	105
Mark J. Mitchell	Ash Wednesday	106
	Out of Sea	107
Ralph Monday	Soliloquy Sacrament	108
	The Hawk's Quill	110
	Owl Woman	111
	Listen to the Ground	112
	Going from Colorado	113

George Moore	Olive Trees, Alto Alentingo	115
	Unwanted Origami	117
	Kola, Oblast	119
Heidi Morrell	Kingdom of the Sea	121
	Waters that Move	123
	Spine of Continents	124
Kacper Niburski	A Nicer Person than Me	125
	Fossil Fuel	126
Suzanne O'Connell	The Patron Saint	127
Mary C. O'Malley	Song of the Sea Wanderer's Wife	129
Carl Palmer	Chambers Creek	130
Simon Perchik	Untitled	121
Richard King Perkins II	So Fleetingly	132
	Water in Louisiana	133
	My Fire at Dawn	135
Freya Pickard	Elemental Haiku	137
Tim Roberts	Corrections and Clarifications	138
Francesca Sasnaitis	Keep Still While Storms Flatten Mountains	140
	Valéry on the Beach	142
Emily Jo Scalzo	Untitled	144

Keenan Schott	The Elements of Palling Around	145
Belinda Singleton	Elemental	146
J.J. Steinfeld	A Hundred Paper Rivers	147
Emily Strauss	Pulling Up the Light	148
Linda Strever	Amelia Earhart Flies at Night	149
	Ebb Tide at Woodard Bay	151
Marianne Szlyk	The Library of Air	152
	At the Library of Water	153
Barbara Tate	Nighttime Accomplice	155
Peter Taylor	The Masons	157
Sarah Thursday	Love Letter No. 4: To the Nail Biter	159
	Oceans Once Receded	160
Jari Thymian	My Curiosity is a Frigate	162
	Looking at Phainopepla	163
Dennis Trujillo	Like a Shift Leader in a Gold Mine	164
Susan Vespoli	Sea Otters	165
Claire Walker	Unbalancing	166
Loretta Diane Walker	Flood	167
	Falling into Morning	168
Connie K Walle	A Look is the Fire Itself	169

Mercedes Webb-Pullman	Spanish Leather	170
	Ruapehu	171
J.R. West	Ghost Dancing	172
	Incompatible	174
Mary L. Westcott	Angelfish	175
	Ode to the Blue Spirit Retreat, Costa Rica	176
Shannon Connor Winward	At the Party Tonight	177
	Remembrance	178
	Maybe the Kindling Brings It On Herself	179
Diana Woodcock	Where Weighty Glaciers Recede	180
Kirby Wright	Waiting for Rain During the Drought	182
Xanadu	Li Na (李娜) Sonnet	183
Mantz Yorke	Brocken, Helm Craig	184
Changming Yuan	Fire	185
	Wood	186

From the Editors

A.J. Huffman	Walking with Wings	189
	An Unscheduled Change in Persona	190
	Lake Huron Rocks	191

	The Path	192
	Spring Released	193
	I Am Leaf	194
	Daily Downpour	196
	The Signs of Spring	197
	The Cold Hand of Winter	198
April Salzano	*December, 2013*	199
	Goodbye September	200
	It's Just What We Do (Winters Up North)	201
	For One Son	202
	Smelling God	203
	Smelling Stinkbug	204
	I Am Going to Kick April's Ass	205
	July and My Mother's Twin	206
	The Day was Buried	207
	Author Bios	211
	About the Editors	233

Featured Piece

This anthology's featured piece represents the editors' choice for the best artistic interpretation of the theme of elements (earth, air, fire, water), and for that reason, the editors feel it deserves special focus.

Personal Geology

My life laid out like this land—
ridges and basins, valleys
filled with silt, narrow channels
cut into layers of red and yellow
sandstone, gullies invisible
from the surface, cliff faces

crumbling with every rain.
I am sliced and uplifted too,
layers of ancient sea mud overlaid
with floods leaving rounded stones
in river beds, drifting wind-borne
sand across hardened shores

fractured by massive forces
that twist and fold pure rock.
My history is evident—
the ground blown clean, plateaus,
washes all visible to the naked eye,
read me like a text in past tense,

millennia of growth and decay,
advance and retreat of oceans
until today. Now I am scarred,
weathered to red spires
forged by wind and rain into shapes
unknown in any nightmare.

See me if you walk here long enough,
feel me beneath your feet like a spring
feeding clear streams where tiny fish
survive their isolation, warm
enough to keep me satisfied in winter
even without your cold embrace.

-- Emily Strauss

From The Authors

Silicon

Aerolite sounds like a comfort shoe brand,
but moonlights as meteorite.
Mother of silicon—you gifted me siblings
in airy quartz, amethyst, star-banded firmament.
Doula to feldspar, mica, clay
Oh my relatives
now I understand Lakota's prayer.
Your secrets buried deep in oceanic plates
whispered on the lips of diatoms
stored in cell walls,
use me as you need to
fortify us for the journey.

Now I understand Lakota's prayer
why you brought me to this valley in my eighteenth year
far from my homeland
so I could marry salt and river, sea and desert wash
so I might trace my birth in red clay earth
silhouetted in charcoal dust
my story spelled out on the neon lips of ocotillos
like mute hands singing.

-- *Sandra Anfang*

Blood of the Soil

I pour red wine onto sun-baked beds
of iris, rose and golden globe. Blue jade
vines swing from a pink tulip tree shading
the bronze Buddha that sits in peace
on a platform of river stones. The garden
is still but for leaves shimmying to the jazz
of morning wind. My offering is silent,
grateful, an opening to elements' blessing,
to the vibrant love that is nature. Feeling
cloudless, the earth having swallowed my feet,
I am planted deep as bitterroot. I breathe in
vast space and the colors of enchantment,
lean toward the Buddha. He gives me a light.

-- Carol Alena Aronoff

In a Time of Drought

reflections of moon on water seem more substantial.
Bird wings sound percussive against the crackle
of dry air. The wisdom of ocean wends its way
through remaining tide pools, offering small currents
in lieu of rain. Wind paints lava in shells and seaweed.
The elements mingle in timeless embrace.

But still no downpour, no clouds to break
the monotony of azure sky. Parched streambeds
moan as toads move slowly seeking respite
from sun. Roots cry out for moisture, gardenias droop,
heads bowed as they pray for rain. Branches
creak, offering solace to wilting leaves, to weary

hummingbirds flitting about in search of nectar.
There is sorrow in this withering landscape,
retreat for some into dormancy or death.
Still, in this time of scarcity and uncertainty,
fruit trees bear more fruit. Nature knows
the way of things.

-- Carol Alena Aronoff

Across The Ether

It took our three brave travelers the best part of two days to reach the Moon in the good ship "Rosamund". This gave them each plenty of time to seriously dent the stock of port, brandy and salted pork packed neatly into leather-strapped hampers by their wives and butlers; and also time to regale each other with exaggerated tales of earlier adventures beneath the sea, in humid jungles or atop snow-crested mountains.

Touchdown was a little bumpy but they were European gentlemen of good breeding so would not complain of a gentle bruising to the worsted-clothed legs and cotton-clad lower backs.

Herbert was first out of his seat, rushing off to the cloakroom and re-emerging five minutes later sporting a rather fetching bathing costume of a blue and white hooped design.

"Can't we do *un peu* sightseeing first?" asked Jules.

"You know I like to build up a healthy appetite with a spot of vigorous exercise. Sea of Tranquility, here I come."

"I'll get the door for you," offered the third man, William, known as Godwin.

The inventor busied himself with the ingenious locking mechanism of the outer door. Highly polished brass mortises clicked and the Morris & Co cushion protected wood moved gently outward. Godwin felt his breath catch in his throat. Shaking his head just slightly, he gently closed the door and turned back to face his companions.

"Reminds me of Kilimanjaro," he opined. "It's, I would say, a touch airless."

Herbert looked crestfallen but Jules twirled his moustache and smiled. "I have just ze ting in ze hold: a breathing apparatus designed by a sea *capitaine* of my acquaintance. In fact, anticipating zis problem, I have three of the devices."

"Capital!" Herbert exclaimed.

Each helped the other into the backpack which was styled in the form of a giant conch shell with a rubber hose attached. Godwin pulled open the door. The Sun was now up on the lunar surface and at first the crystalline twinkling gave the impression of dappled water in front of them. But it was soon proven to be an illusion akin to the stage exploits of Monsieur Mesmer.

"*Sacre bleu*," cursed Jules. "The Sea of Tranquility is –"

"Mere dust," Herbert interrupted.

"With the odd, reflective rocky shard and occasional crater," Godwin beamed. "I shall fetch a spade and a magnifying lens forthwith."

Herbert pursed his lips, aware that he'd been foolish enough to trust his own scientific suppositions and thus lay a bet with his fellow explorer; consequently, he would now be out of pocket to the tune of five guineas. The surface curved away to the horizon – craters like dried-up geysers; loose grey-brown rocks scattered across the otherwise smooth lake of… dust. What a disappointment. They wandered around for a few minutes, leaving footprints that would cause some consternation in later centuries, there being no space breeze to shift and reform the topsoil.

Back inside the good ship "Rosamund", Herbert continued to bemoan his fortune: "We made this journey across the ether for… well, for nothing. I could have taken tea with the Prime Minister down in Brighton… and dipped my toes in the English Channel on Sunday after church."

"That sea belongs to France ," Jules corrected, giving his companion a hearty slap on the back. "But fear not, my Anglais friend," he announced, "I have been doing some calculations for our next adventure."

"Yes...?" said the two others.

"Well, we would need to cut down our intake of ham, *rosbif*, quail's eggs and dry sherry."

"Sir!" Herbert responded. "We are gentlemen of science, not Spartans or penitents."

Godwin pulled a fountain pen and a sheet of narrow feint paper from his jacket pocket and commenced a hasty set of algorithms. "I think I can guess Monsieur Jules's intentions," he stated. "It would mean dining a little more frugally. And only three times a day."

"Harrumph!" Herbert evacuated.

"Merci for your support, Godwin. So, young Herbert, I have calculated that we have enough fuel to re-route from here. A little detour to the red planet."

"Capital!" Herbert beamed. "I've always dreamed of Mars. And I'll get my swim in after all – in one of their many canals."

-- *Allen Ashley*

Bee Lake

Every few years the rivers jumped
and spread out over the land.
When they receded we found new forms
scratched out of black earth.
Lakes shaped like rivers,
new streams, slow and full.
Bee Lake was formed that way.

The Yazoo carried on its shoulders
carcasses of animals
that had drowned in the flood.
It was too crowded with stinking
death and too slender to swim or ski.

So for Bee Lake, farmers
hauled out tons of sand
for building a beach we had to share
with one frustrated bull and his cows.

The bottom was black silt mud
spiked with the tops of sharp stems.
Water moccasins sunned on the broke
black trees on the banks and grew fat.

I faced forward in the boat,
my face waterbeaten,
wind smearing my silly smiles
with women of 16 & 18 and older boys.
Learning the smoke dance of beery lips,
Vantage cigarettes, serious
steamy eyes, singing laughter
in raining mouths and slurs.
In the evening the steel rimmed sky,
grayed over the blue with thousands of bats.

-- Harvey J. Baine

The Grudge

Like a lone duck breaking
the smooth surface of a pond,
a grudge nags at still waters,
causing deep disturbances below,
jiggling water weeds, shifting dark sands.
No gentle lapping of shoreline,
no peaceful reflections.
Instead, concentric circles spread
in all directions, wider and wider—
just as the delicate flutter of butterfly wings
can change atmospheric air currents
into destructive tornadoes.

-- Barbara Bald

The Wind Notices the Season

green barley chases itself towards the gorse
on its hill - goes upwards and glances sideways
as directed by the wind as if in a game

has no rules to be kept or mastered
only the seasons will change what happens
or when the barley has been harvested

later grazed upon and the gorse will
not be in heavy bloom - its yellow
so like broom except for the thorns

neither are cut but sometimes burned
though never up there amongst the stones
where their bulk dominates paths

below each bush between each rock
not made by man - burrows can
sport solid roofs and sound from the wind

broom has the softer stems and stays
further down where everything else
feels the rush of movement too

-- James Bell

The Bent Air

Just as swift, the air that clings to light's moving
form turns cold,
hard and bent and ready to break.
Yet, there is nothing to hold on to in
such a set body,
but compound of diesel
fuel and spikes of acid rain.
A salvaged smell.
Reminds one of those memories lumbering upon
the ill-used tracks,
with miles and miles of telephone poles
strung by rubber-coated wires,
stretching long on either side of the tubes,
and no blinking lights to put on guard
for careless idlers.
All appear nevertheless false,
the way clarity ghosts its pale back through
the quiet scenery,
and wards the mortal world from the bent
dregs of air that feeds on itself.

-- Lana Bella

The Dry Bone

The field has gone along without rain
a dry bone in a drier season—
it lay downtrodden besides the sloping dell under a
thick valance of breathless mist,
tasting the decayed rust perching on its parched tongue;
the air unfurled like embers from a searing fire:
rising, tumbling, bouncing, then all at once,
drooping in ashy dew towards the fracture-mottled
ground and stirring the few scurried beings
down below the cracked
bedrock floor;
its sorrow tottered on fragile stumps,
weaving with care between loose pellets clay
and swarming flies,
clutching the last brown leaf in its palmed bruised hand
as the earth was once more, coursed with flames.

-- Lana Bella

Emily Dreaming

Emily dreams—in water—
The cemetery—her pool.
Looking out on Amherst's green—
She swims—in liquid cool.

It's true she's dressed—in gossamer!
Her gills look more like wings.
She deftly strokes the water.
The pen beside her sings—

A lovely tune in ink and chains
On paper—pillow—bones.
And in her dreams—her nightly laps—
With ink—and death—and poems—

-- Nancy Boutilier

The Uncle Whose Only Daughter Died

He's out by the loud river again confounded
that the forecast was right
rain hitting heavy

which means he has to unpack
his camera by hand from underneath

the hood of his slicker, head bent,
hunched. Behind him is tomorrow's photo

of a rock-shocked waterfall in tiers
that sometimes through thick spray offers up
iris-colored tatters

a Killarney rainbow in pieces

so he has to keep shielding lenses
and dials from splatter until that last
split-second prayer

of aim, focus, pre-set flash
I've seen the violence

of his torso-twisting around and tail-spinning
the Nikon in both hands—

he shoots—

       and before it gets wet twists back
to that same waterproof doubling-over

then yells at any exposure
gone bad

like some fugitive from behind bars
who when finally stabbed in the gut wails
a Christ-damning oath from the slush.

                -- Therese Broderick

Holy Fire Painting with Yves Klein

-- after *Peinture feu couleur sans titre*, artist Yves Klein, 1962

Fire retardant
The female form
Masking the flames
Leaving a negative
Impression on paper

A figure emerges
On the canvas
A phoenix rising
From the edges
In a burnt embrace

-- Tanya Bryan

Harpyiai

I shall wear the name *harpy* as armour – it is no insult
to be Aellai. I am no gust – I hit the dirt hard, I am
a hurricane. Open my mouth and spit typhoons, snatch
up your frowns, turn them in my twists. Only a bloke
could wax such words about ugliness – as if only the kind
are beautiful, only the fair of face are allowed to be loved.

Who has sat you man, as judge of our worth? No wonder
I rattle the air in my wings – spread them, knock you flat
with backdraft, fly you a face-full of feathers. See my body –
my skin is prickle sprout, my legs were a spatchock as I pushed
my baby out. My wild-horse child, his Anemoi dad busy blowing
the hills about, all bombast. Air is a delicate thing if we leave it alone –

just breathe, nothing more. Y*our voice is sharp*, he says. Beak
ever ready to bite. He does not hear the gentle song I give to the end
of day – he does not see my half-bird body sparrow hop
around supermarkets, peck at the washing line with pegs.
I gave my heart to Boreas – he blew a winter's chill over the landscape
of our love, lapped about our home until it was a seat of ice. Our nest

is lined with frost – we find no comfort in these frigid twigs.
I should cast him to my sisters, born of atmosphere and Earth –
Erinyes, furious at them who did not keep their oaths. I feel them beat
the ground above their heads – *send us your faithless!* I cast my face
to floor, hoping to feel them, cheek on cheek. They shall not call us crones!
Not when we have been hacked and hurt – we are shafts of survival.

We are more dazzling than those men will ever understand.

-- Jane Burn

Joining Forces

Calling It Forth

One immovable
Part of nature; earth cried out
Blaze me, cool me . . . flow!

Elemental Gathering

Earth provided strength
Fire, water danced up high
Uplifted by air

Quieted Corner

Earth and fire marched
Water and air calmed them down
Peace came that evening

On Their Own

Fire scorched its path
Water carved, air moved freely
Only earth stood still

-- Janet Rice Carnahan

United Purpose

Each element came,
Sizing each other's strengths
Balance required

Trail blazing fire
Slowed down to rushing water
Air and stone stilled

Air up, spiraling
Flames escorted high
Water sprung from rock

Bright red fire spit
Cool blue water soothed embers
Sweet night air, dark stone

-- Janet Rice Carnahan

The Elements

They were wannabe
rock stars, prototype
punkettes with spiked
hair, blank eyes, and
voices rasped by razor
blades; Earth, Air,
Wind and Fire on acid.
Claimed they were
three screaming
banshees from Hell
but were actually from
Syosset. Were backed
up by four guys voted
most likely to die of an
overdose by their junior
high classmates.
The drummer losing
a spot for a heavy metal
band gig to a guy who
was rumored to have
spontaneously combusted,
leaving behind nothing but
a signed set of sticks and
a brutally abused cow bell.
Did club dates in places
health inspectors wouldn't
go. Lost fans to characters
straight out of movies like
"Under the Skin" and
"The Hunger." Flamed out
long before their singles went
gold on albums that had
no names as much due to
a lack of interest than

creative differences.
They won't be missed.

> *-- Alan Catlin*

Alchemical Wedding

-- Dedication to Carl McCoy of the Fields of the Nephilim

Magus in temple, you unveil mysteries of the soul
Sacred texts intoned, herald of the new eon of old
Sermons sung are the union of elements revealed to Horus
The Golden Rosy + Cross, the secret symbols are before us

Your order is the link to the original manifestos
Your lodge, the seven ascending steps to wisdom, the source
The Christ dying, descending into the earth
Resurrected and reborn

Distill the vital fluid; extract from my body the salts
Powder of the first projection contain in a metal box
The Hermetist's Gold is a reflection of the gods
A light without shadow reuniting lovers lost

In immortality and glory, my rose unfolds its many petals
Our very labor of love, a King and Queen's chemical wedding

-- Alexis Child

Fire

First brush, the low invaders,
Red maple saplings, poison ivy,
Brier or honeysuckle, then higher
into the canopy, leaping
like bright ideas from birch to pine.
Deciduous to evergreen overlapping
edge of climate and topography.
Red eye of engulfment.

Hell was decreed by this
sort of intensity. Everlasting
as molten gold boiling in the vats
of Vulcan. The great oaks and hickories
withstanding wildfires, their dense hearts
clenched on burl or knot
as resinous balsams burst
into catcalls of flame.

-- Joan Colby

Electrical Fire

Fire springs from wire to wire
Within the infrastructure,
Walls heating with a buried passion
Like a stalker at the windows
Where glass begins its slow melt,
A pulse, pre-orgasmic as the way
Rafters learn how negligible
Their defenses. The balloon construction
Turns architecture to a chimney
Of exaltation. Firefighters
Stand back framed by equipment
Useless to staunch what has overtaken
Tactics. They might as well admire
The nature of such forces, unlike a dream
Forgotten in relief. No. This culminates
In ash, the stone foundations
Blackened the way a man and woman
Declare that it's all over.

-- Joan Colby

The Secret Life of Fire

fire
    was a small child,
hid
    behind pant legs
did
    everything he was told,
watched
    the same thing that made his father crawl into a bottle

fire
    reacted the opposite way
lost
    secrets and subtlety
roars
    with the sound of the sun,
just warms
    when he's tired or far enough away
not to burn

        -- Esteban Colon

Mountain Storm

Cumulonimbus lurking   peering over
white topped peaks   like
childhood's hunchbacked monsters
      waiting   to
pounce as

shadows lick the creviced slopes
      white and green become grey
lights flash behind drawn shades of
ominous clouds

Darkness pours into valleys where
rows of birches waver as if
nervously laughing
on the river shore

Relentlessly advancing the storm
growls and cracks and snaps and
      the landscape disappears behind
wind and rain

God's angry swords slash the dark
      each   plunge deep
with loud report and
all bow at its advance   some
shatter and fall

Gone now   like it never came
still grumbling as it departs
to disturb   more peaceful scenes
beyond the valley

Halfway up the mountainside the
sun plays at the tree line   below
      a more peaceful grey
ushers in the night

              -- Craig Cornish

Just Fishing

the day is colorless   like
    charcoal sketches   almost
one dimensional

I gaze from my perch
at water's edge   looking
beyond my line   which
is taut   and moving   startled

I flick my rod back and
    the line goes limp   but
I leave it there

not thinking   or caring that
the bait might be   gone

I'm not really here to fish anyway

it is only an excuse to
    be alone   and
some might think it strange
to be   just sitting here
    in the rain

                       -- Craig Cornish

Shrouded In Mist

    -- After The Mist Moves In, *photograph by Mark Bright*

The father

tall & tan
in drawstring trunks

watches
her

rise from the waves
two pieces of blue

cinched waist
span of his hands

the daughter

rips away
her cap

hair
furiously free

looks to see
if he sees

her striding
toward him

washing away
footprints

                -- Chella Courington

Late Harvest

I will be called beauty   lapis eyes born
of metamorphic rock   aureoles hot.

I will be desired   for land to raise wheat
abundantly and cattle   for slaughter.

I will be deserted   after seven years unable
to bear his seed   torn and dry.

He will not return   convinced I will not rise
in estrus fully   vulva blooming

pomegranates and grapes   olives and figs
roll down slopes   he once gutted.

-- Chella Courington

Down the Pacific Coast

Waves breaking in chaotic throbs
Heaving wild of winds
    Wild of sea-steeds
        stomping down the path of Jonah
            trailing behind white manes of foam

These racing hooves
    with overt physicality
        churning waters to granite
            and ripping seaweed from a watery song
                bruising the waters with a melody of evermore
                    to ever after

Salt and sand
    Crustaceans and corals
        sinking to the ocean floor
            going down___while remembering
                the look of clouds, the feel of winds

Flukes cutting through waters
and floats mapping a fluid poem
of sails and spinnakers
above a deep of dark

Brine and brackish
Twisting seaweed hands___intertwined
to shift and part the waters.
of oceans with outstretched arms
embracing the earth
    in a consolation for everything lost

Revengeful Ahab
the sea horses Socrates rode to Troy
to capture Homer's mermaids,
    drowning in the surly surf
        of star-shelled nights

Tern of sky
Bulwark of swells
stacking high to watery wall
spilling forth
rolling over everything in its path
trouncing the shores

Sent forth by the word . . . a fluid song of sea and sky
soothed by the sirens' song___
into long rolling lines
breaking around piers
holding lumps of slippery gray,
barking seals

What command given when
To where the wild and whirling winds
    divined an essence of life
that tossed stars into a moon-driven night
and summoned seagulls to voice
screeches above slippery rocks
dipping into cubby holes
hiding nesting crabs and a long-armed squid

Over and around, sea songs of winds and surf
  spawning and birth

What screams in wind-tossed waters
But pleas of sea sirens
Neptune carries them off
In paw-prints of the moon
up a rocky coast
across water tossed stones
slippery bare

Deep of tides
gathering to bathe jeweled anemones
and one pink starfish

Oysters in one nest, crabs in another
Neighbors waiting for a command
in voice heard only by ocean ears

Barnacles clinging to rocks of slip and wet
and troops of turtles carried out to sea.

-- Susan Dale

Of Earth

Earth of pollen and stamens
Of walls breathing in
Breathing out
With an expanding universe
Seeing with dim eyes, the spines
That hold up the nights
bending under the weight of our dreams

Dreams following a dim light
to the very edge of consciousness

There's another light
This one cascades over shadows
And over the earth of silences
accumulating
In the segments we split

Earth of circles and chains
Of hands groping for the moon
Of bloodless hearts
Of stone souls
Of our blind feet
Stumbling down the path of being

-- Susan Dale

Tibetan Prayer Flags

Blue sky white wind red fire
green water yellow earth:
five flags repeating themselves
like a mystical chant,
the wind horses at center
galloping in line from shrine
to mountain outcrop,
the only sound the train
crossing the roof of the world,
Han settlers in oxygenated cars
dismissing the spiritual laundry
as they hurtle on toward
the lure of capitalized Lhasa.

-- Chip Dameron

Days Without Anger -- Day 7

Rain on a metal roof in Pennsylvania
is a different beast than in Colorado or New Mexico.

Rain on a metal roof before an orgasm
is a different beast than during or after.

Rain rain rain for six days passes like an arrow
loosed by a naked hunter needing to feed her family.

Rain on forever is a different beast
on which to build a lifetime without anger.

-- Theresa Darling

After The Deluge (c'est nous)

After a day of frustration Marjorie finally upended a bucket of water, drained from one of the garden butts, over her husband.

The water was cold and in other circumstances might have been thought refreshing on that sultry summer evening. It was also green and full of nutrients from having filtered through the moss and detritus on the slated roof of the double garage. It might, cascading over Peter's head and shoulders, staining his white chinos and soaking his red-check Oxford shirt, have broken the tight spell of the argument that had simmered between them in the late July heat, but which had not yet erupted. It might have caused them to stop and look, and to dissolve into storms of laughter as once, many years before, they might have done.

As it was Peter strove to respond with dignity, silently turning his head towards her and then, as if seeing her for the first time, rising slowly from his chair and moving away, as one might move from an encroaching shadow.

She watched him go, a trail of water darkening the flagstones behind him; running water around his chair, diminishing to water footprints as he traversed the terrace and entered the house by the conservatory doors.

When he had gone she felt suddenly ridiculous, still holding the upside-down bucket, standing at the edge of a pointless sheet of ebbing water. She set the bucket down on the stone slabs and glanced from side to side, as if fearing that hidden friends might jump out from the bushes to surprise her. Then she did not know what to do. She felt alone. She could not bring herself to look upwards towards the upstairs windows. She wanted to tell him that he had deserved it, but she could not explain, even to herself, what it had been.

She had done something absurd, and perhaps irrevocable. No. Something that was undoubtedly irrevocable. Already it was something in their joint past that neither could escape from. It might be forgiven; it could not be forgotten , and it could never be undone. They would forever be defined by it. He would be the man whose wife had, one day without warning, tipped a bucket of water over him. She would be the woman who had done such a thing. Wherever they went, separately or together, that would be who they were.

In fun? People would ask, and the tellers of the tale would tilt their heads and pull faces that suggested ambiguity. But it had not been in fun. It had been without all humor. Even now she could not see the funny side.

And that was what it had revealed to her.

She wondered if Peter would come back out onto the terrace, and if he did, what he would be wearing, and what he would say. She stood looking out over the lawn, which was two steps down from the terrace, from which the water still dripped onto the parched grass.

-- Brindley Hallam Dennis

Four Elements of Woman

Earth: The Teenager

She is made of folk-lore & fairy tales, a woman living in the woods
running alongside deer, among them, within them.
She drags her feet through the leaves, crunching them like bones,
hobbling like Wallace's cripple in autumn. She's been cut deep &
her scars bear deep across her throat. But she knows now, how deep inside
she really has to go to die. In healing, she has built thick skin for winter
gathered provisions, and prepared. She touches her scar & echoes to the skyline
I can survive.

Water: The Therapist

She is half-made of shadows, & underground shells,
believing the best in the worst of us, pulling others up from the ground
where the rain gathered in the ditch & made their skin stitch like mud
with strangers fever dreams that leave teeth marks on pillow cases.
She understands how to drain oceans of their contents to search for
whales without being stuck inside of one. She is no Jonah; she answers to no man.
All rivers lead downstream, where salmon spawn & she catches them with her jaw
in the calm, she makes sure the sea inside her mouth goes nowhere.
She waits out the silence; she wades out into bodies of water
& wears a starfish around her throat, to remind herself she's better than
a siren, and if needed, she can bloom new limbs having been sliced.

Fire: The Reporter

The next woman is quixotic, made of fire colored curls
on her head & covered with a chameleon's skin, nearly burned
to a crisp with freckles & sun sickness. She can cut off her tongue
in an argument, but grow a new one by noon. Her fingers move to fast
to be caught, and her head is filled with smoke from the words & stories
& other people she has yet to be. She will not be caught.
Worst of all, she knows it. Nothing like a forest fire
with agency & self awareness. We will all be charred and burned by morning--
blink--then read about our own destruction in third person in the morning paper.
Fire cannot be contained. You may put it out, but it is never gone. She moves beyond
hearth, beyond earth, and lives inside the flame. She only gives first names, while
double checking all her sources.

Air: The Reject

The clouds bore the next woman, wearing white & shaped like a pearl.
She enters once & that is enough to know she is not wanted.
She does not need to scrape her knees, begging faceless men,
again and again, in order to get up. If she stays down, she knows
how to navigate back into the air. Her teeth are tiny. Her words are meek.
But she rides horses at dawn & dusk, to prepare herself for a storybook ending
& riots. She is made of words, empty letter containers that empty out their remainders
of meaning when the next person comes along. In a room alone, she sits
and hangs heavy. Queer, like Alice in the book she read as a child.
She remembers her legacy, ripped & hollowed out by her circumstance.
She is invisible, until it rains. Then
the clouds part, sunlight comes through, creating a rainbow;
an art project without a frame. Air is invisible until it wants to be
then beauty will pass through it and to the other side. The woman of the air
is quiet, too until she learns to take the insults from the sidelines
break apart her mirrored image & thrive.

-- Evelyn Deshane

Slow Motion

Clouds wait like battleships
in a sea of blue,
spotting the surface
with shadows.

The battleship flotilla
with their attendants
point grimly to
an unknown destination.

Shadows,
grey shapes
like stingrays
in a sandy inlet

circle and hound
the convoy
and the clouds
slowly slip

unnoticed
over the horizon.

-- Eric Dodson

Eating Local

To eat what grows at the edge of the tall grass,
I'd have to be a bison, maybe a mustang grazing,
running with the herd in the spring wind,
winter coats shedding out. Coyote with a rabbit,
or prairie dog feeding on tough Indian grass.

Instead, I sit in Cafe Luna facing a full plate
of mesclun greens, egg and artichoke pie, imported
black olives, Earl Grey tea with milk and honey.

The bees are dying. Maybe the eggs make sense.
Ravenous, I broil, boil, braise and grill the world,
sliced and skewered, eat our common sunlight and rain.

-- Karen Douglass

Urgedanke

that darkness, the immaterial
being before time
a world created
in a state of four
geometric, balanced
chiseled out as words

the black bile of earth
dry as autumn, melancholic
the dissolute mountains fall
an inevitable tectonics
a slow shattering
of stone

the carefree air, cloud ground
wing space, there
all movement is joy
and when the wind blows
we call it love

at the horizon
the intersection of states
a meridian of fire
where the idea inflames
is a human blade and all blood
becomes inferno

then the cooling water
that douses all such
conflagrations with reason
gentle as snow but in which
we may also drown
our flesh dissolved

now the moment of hydrogen
where we breed ourselves

in suns, circle
within a circle
we build a table with its bones
and create a priesthood

all around the fire we sing
of making, shadow melody
cast out into the darkness
up they fly, our words
like sparks, brief
and blazing

urstoff
unheimlich

-- morgan downie

Author's note: urgedanke - primal thinking/concept
urstoff - primal material/stuff
unheimlich - uncanny (from freud)

Transcendence

Glow of approaching cars exposes
Front glass' scattered abrasions
Seals them with time
Never-ending new-old destinations
Previews of fantasy
Deceived by past memory
And darkness
    Light
                And darkness
Fire's tongue is gently licking white petals
Thick fog of mystical dreams sings spirit song
Wild berries' black juice stains oak cup
Wings of an eagle are breaking the thunder's circle
Ancestral whispers
Healing chants
Drums gather a sunrise
Winds of time
Lost
                Between worlds

-- Inna Dulchevsky

Small Star Poem

At first
on the glass
the rain drop
seems tense

then
the urge
to crowd
overwhelms—

it   pulls
collects another
to draw a line
in time
through space
downward

a small star
in a meager heaven
has spent itself

at last.

-- J.K. Durick

Fire

In a world aflame
with states ablaze
whole forests and
city blocks burning
my car going up
is next to nothing.

I feel the nothing
of flames and smoke,
I smell the nothing
of plastics and fabrics,
raging out of control,
the burning blackness
of it – till the windows
pop, one at a time, till
the strain and stress of
it all seems almost epic.

For a few seconds my
ten year old car is
the center of a small
universe – a driveway,
a street, a few neighbors.
There is a force and
beauty in its going.

This was the street.
This was its driveway.
These were the neighbors
who watched it come
and go and thought
very little of it all.

Now they see it, feel
the heat of its going,
hear the hissing and

the popping, smell it,
and probably taste it.
This is center stage,
the center of awareness,
a lesson about endings.

-- J.K. Durick

Dinner after the Storm

At 6:00 the greenish sky, taupe, purple as a cape
looses its torrents amidst crash & splintering and then is spent.
Our shadows drenched & drowned. Orange & crimson swords
pierce a loitering cloudbank. I see you, Mother,
wield your dripping lance.

Candles center the table, afloat in your crystal bowl.
Flames waver from waxen boats, cast trapezoids
& secret triangles upon the water. Your tomato wheels
layer a plate, their clean-sliced surfaces like lambent moons
in a cloud-tailed sky. Our one moon rises.

Sky had hung, heavy as a clothesline sheet.
Wind had gusted, loam in the nose, a sudden chill.
Something of rain & wind still clings to these tomatoes, buoyant,
clear as an evening transparent with release.
Pairs of lungs in their cut surfaces.
Water-wings that let us float.

You have cleared away the clutter. You, Mother, old
regulator of clouds: your tomatoes an almanac, our tidal chart.

                     -- Lucia Galloway

After the Eruption

The leaves—
ash

the trunks—
black

the rocks—
blasted

the air—
poisoned

at the center:
a gaping crater
shaped like a heart.

-- Brigitte Goetze

Northern Woman

She wears even in summer
heavy boots and lumber jacket
that make her easy to spot
each lunchtime when she feeds
squirrels and chases pigeons.
"Filthy city buggers," she says and
stamps her boots
but the pigeons don't budge.
They know her hunting days are over.

In her room
hands that baited traps and scraped hides
open another bottle and
pull the curtains to stop the neon lights.
"Nothing's out there," she mutters
and turns to face a photo
of herself, her man and bear-skin stretched between them.
They had known the warmth of great animals.

At the river early
before freeway traffic starts
she catches a bucket of bass puny
fed by what the city does not want.
She picks up an old pike
left on the sand
too stiff to swim again
its gills still quiver.
"Dead or alive. One or the other."
She whacks the fish against a rock
silver slimes its open eye.

Home rocking, she looks with eyes open
at her man and bear shrunk to the size of the frame.
"One or the other," she whispers.

-- Joan Goodreau

Flight Plan

Lost little hummingbird
darting within the cypress
seeking life from color, yet,
all about is vibrant green.

Too much energy expended chasing the airy life,
while the fat house cats watch from the window.

-- Rick Hartwell

Storm

The storm is a dress
the world carefully opens
and brilliantly removes.

But tonight,
as we peal apart,
the lightning fading
with the blush of thundering blood
that will leave your face pale,

the storm wears the earth
like a lover she's peeling away;
the earth still orbiting, not knowing
where the storm went.

-- H. Edgar Hix

Mitigation

Squeezed between buildings,
even this man-made wetland,
a scummed pond and a water-
meadow flecked with the detritus
of hundreds of lunches, has attracted
red-winged blackbirds who nest in the reeds,
a great blue heron stalking the water's edge
and shiny endangered turtles,
smaller than the span of your hand.

-- Ruth Holzer

Breathing

Once in a while
I must take down
from a high shelf
the lightweight blue
wind-and-waterproof back-
pack with the chevrons
of reflective gray,
the shoulder-harness
and waist-straps
      dangling engagingly,
buckles and zippers
tinkling like distant bells,
inner pockets holding
particles of glass and shale.
I lift out a wad of maps
from the very bottom
and plunge my head deep inside
to breathe again that rare
air of the North Atlantic.

-- Ruth Holzer

In the Japanese Garden

Not a belt but a pocket
of green serenity
amid urban sprawl.

Like its namesake beetle
the garden glistens,
chartreuse, harlequin, teal.
Moss, reed, pine.
No flower excites the eye.
Plant, stone, earth
Muffle city sound.

Water murmurs.
No one speaks.
Tranquil
until the turtle
plops into the pond--
nature's exclamation point.

-- Liz Hufford

The Elements

sun
cannot remove
mud
from my doorsill:
all
that it can do:
bake
the moisture
out:
turn it into
dust:
it takes a solemn
wind
to blow the dust
away:
or seed a river
longing
for the sea.

-- W. Luther Jett

Golem

Out of solid
    earth, a hand
scratching at the sky.

Do you, who scatter
    ashes, understand
what is written there?

A small bird   could carry
this riddle;   the wild sea
    reveals.

From the roiling
    waves, gushes
a fire dark as my blood.

-- W. Luther Jett

Moon Sleep

I stick
my hand
out toward
the sea,
roll out my palm.
I offer a plank,
a trail for you to follow
into the salty stars,
where you stretch out
and give your heart
to this final moment
of the glass night sky;
draw me in—
sketch my face
on the edge
of a wave—
over ages of celestial
moon sleep and dust.

-- Michael Lee Johnson

Lost in a Distant Harbor

Love,
once beside me

now

lost in a
distant harbor

calls out into the night
crawls back into the fog.

-- Michael Lee Johnson

Returning

Copper leaves crunch,
crisp around my feet.

The night returns,
burnt from the sun.

The sky crumbles,
time contracts,

feathered flight over
forest and gulch.

Memories of you
turning to mulch.

-- Lori Kiefer

Sky Note

Out at dawn,
I walk along
the Stroud Green Road,
searching for significance.
Thin white stripes
curve the sky
like a cotton tea cozy.
A flick of birds
forms a message,
feather-wrapped
and stamped.

I imaging my name
is on it.

-- Lori Kiefer

Danger

The electricity
between the kite
and the fingers
of my little son's hands.

*   *   *

The overhead lines
beckoning the colours
we'd painted on the sail.

*   *   *

My eyes
fire brigades
as the breeze
tangles the kite in trees.

-- Noel King

To the River of Flame

*"There are the doors
you see with an inner eye:
the moment you pull up
a flower and fear
the ground has opened up for you"*

-- Heidi Hatt

It wasn't the man or god
in his black robes
forearms
bulging, eyes
gone red with flecks

of gold
or his night-tar
stallions
heaving their weight
through spring

fields -
neither passion
nor strength
 not imperviousness
to struggle

or screams, but the
 pull
of that flower,
red
and black, mysterious

that stone
door
marked with flame
torn open
in the rain-soaked earth.

          -- Steve Klepetar

Balm in the Wind

Throaty gasps of
"love, love,"
that balm in the wind.

If a man stumbled down golden
steps to the world's shining
rim, If he opened wounded

hands and felt the vinegar sting
of air, If he spoke softly
in a language made of glass,

If he crept panther-like
in the brush, bearing a tree
filled with nests, would we hear

his whispering as nothing
but the same three words muttered
again and again under steamy breath?

-- Steve Klepetar

Sailboats on the Beach

White sail blades merge with creamy
cloud smear, sky a shade less blue

than echoing sea. In the background's
deep haze, gray sails, ghost boats

bobbing at the edge of sight, whisper
what we already know: that everything

seen in this sweet image feels lighter,
presses more gently on the frozen heart.

Beached boats, open to the eye, clean
curved, sliced red melons, show

nothing of bilge or barnacles or rust.
White hint of gull twisting low above

masts, yellow and slate-blue, riggings
of oak and green-brown rope, anchor dug

in burnished sand. A boat named "Amitie"
leans out toward gentle sea. Not a soul

in sight, or only soul. Sky peels back, layer
by thin layer, pale and paler white until the eye

is blind. The sky is whiter than an eye, ringed
red with tiny veins. Here sailboats fly free

of anchor, curve like sweeping gulls, trace
long lines of flight, careen wildly in dazzled air.

-- Steve Klepetar

Strike Anywhere

It was sunny so they rowed to the middle of the lake. Ida took her clothes off—"I want an even tan"—and Marvin wasn't sure if he was supposed to look, but the white barrel of her stomach annoyed him. Such an exhibitionist, he thought.

"You look too warm in that jacket," Ida hinted.

"I'm fine," Marvin said. He recalled the one time they had made love, a year ago, in the dark, during an electrical storm. Under the covers, her breasts felt huge. Here in the sun, they looked flat and saggy and they lolled like two ling cod on the refrigerator shelf of her stomach. He let the rowboat drift.

And maybe they had eaten spaghetti that night. A pot of tomato sauce on the burner had bubbled up lava-like and spattered the white enamel stovetop with alarming red droplets that could have been blood or anything. Long noodles and penetration frightened him. In the morning, while Ida made cinnamon toast, Marvin said he hoped they could return to being friends.

"You mean Platonic?" Ida asked.

"If that means skip the sex, you bet," Marvin said.

Ida shrugged. In fact she shrugged out of her robe and continued making cinnamon toast naked.

Now, here they were again, albeit in a rowboat, with her naked and him wondering where his life was going. He stood up. The boat rocked so that sky and water and trees tilted wildly, as if the world didn't know which way to go, as if he were on one of the carnival rides that terrified him as a child. He reached for Ida. She squinted up and raised one arm, limp, as if to forgive or invite or engulf. "Marvin," she breathed. He grabbed her armpits and hauled her over the side—over the *gunnel*, which was a word he learned from his scout leader on a day the whole troop had come to this very lake to fish, a day on which the scout leader kept singling out Marvin for humiliation, as when Marvin read from

the scout manual and pronounced it "gun-wale." "*Gunnel*," the man hollered, his red face close to Marvin's.

Now Ida sank, head down, private parts up, fading under the algal murk. As the world went dark, a bright memory flared: she was five years old and a neighbor's house went up in flames, combusted all at once, the whole house, and, for the first time in fifty years, she remembers the Diamond "Strike Anywhere" matches she and her brother Anselm stole that morning from their mother's stovetop, all that power pressed into the red tips, nestled in the slide-out box like rows of rubies.

-- Andrea Lewis

Fire

so many nights in our new
apartment over A&P with
its machines and valves and
heaters, smoke began to
fill the one hall down stairs,
certainly not built to code
with only one way out. My
sister and I in our pajamas
waited on Main Street in
our slippers while our
parents held us close.
Usually it was a small fire,
put out fast and we trudged
back up stairs to bed, the
smell of smoke lingering for
days. Soon the fires in my
life got bigger. Each time the
sirens began, my mother
called Dan, a friend and phone
operator to check out where
the trouble was. In a small
town, everyone knew where
everything was happening.
You could just dial operator
and he'd know. My mother
began checking the house each
night before she turned off
the lights. "Don't put anything
too close to the radiator,"
we were warned. It was better
when the grocery store
became a bookstore. But then
on the night I went to see
the ballet movie Coppelia, on
the way home that scary noise
began. This time it was the

high school, burnt to the ground.
All my books and my science
project, a cashmere sweater I
left in my locket. This wasn't like
a snow day when everyone
cheered and knew we'd be back
to normal. This was the end of
where David smiled at me on the
stairs. I can't say I was sorry
to see the horrid gym where I
I sat all one hideous sock dance
waiting to be asked to dance.
We had class at the college for
the rest of the year which wasn't
bad with its dark mahogany and
stuffed exotic birds in glass cases. A
few years later, my uncle's storage
room, full of my old science projects,
sequin gowns, paintings of horses—
all went up in smoke. I was in
college by then and didn't know
what I'd have done with a gigantic
papier mache model of the eye,
but still….My mother never left the
house without going back more
miles to make sure she hadn't left
a cigarette burning. She never
had but it was a ritual until finally,
too late, she gave them up. I've
loved candles and bon fires,
chocolate melted over a flame but
I still have, as I did in chemistry,
trouble striking a match

-- Lyn Lifshin

Ephram Pratt Remembers Time in the Garden

Climbing the acorns of despair,
he reached into his pocket

and found sand,
sand the color of air,

clear, clean & drenched
in wisps of salt peter

and wine vinegar,
adding a strange luscious

quality to whatever
he mistook for reality.

Dangerous it was,
like wielding a cutlass

in the Garden of Eden,
softening the reach

of time as it flowed
into his slim silence,

guarding a mound of
blackberry bushes

growing in silence
behind the house on Mason,

like a glowing coal,
burnt into soft molasses.

-- Jack e Lorts

Ephram Pratt Sings to the Sun

Raising his hands
into the sky

as silver ball bearings
beat onto the roof,

filtering silence
into soft lightning,

guarding the sound of air
as it pulses

into a forged nightmare,
a lynch pin of desire.

Let it sink quietly
into the west

as fire spreads
over the horizon,

spreads into a nightmare
of wilting incense,

casting wide fingers
into the wind,

seeking rain drops
to challenge

a cacophony of silence
as it belies the willowy

days of late summer,
excelsior playing in the distance.

-- Jack e Lorts

Aphrodite Rides the Bus

she goes where she likes
anywhere she goes it rains
as she brings this weather with her
when the hydraulic doors bump and hiss she steps
through a curtain of falling water

so that her skin glistens
so that her hair tangles
so that her shapely feet become
small splashing cymbals
with   each   wet   step

she arrives at your door
insinuates herself into your awareness
like most women
slip into a pair of sheer stockings
she slides into your subconscious

down the spiral staircase of your soul
her hands inside yours her limbs your inner scaffold
you shed your outerself
walk naked and unashamed
through the crowded streets of your dreams

-- Hillary Lyon

Fleurs du Feu

what a gift you have given me
hot smell of perfumed skin
kissed dropping like melted wax
in pools of radiating colors
a conflagration of hungry petals and stems
devouring the dry flesh of my days
rendering my life into so much
kindling
what a gift you've laid
on this table between us a bouquet
of brightly burning shadows
at once decimating
and delicious

-- Hillary Lyon

To a Drill Bit, Now a Bookend

    -- for CFL

Iron flower   curled and tarnished
by relentless churning
through the hard
secretive earth—

a fierce fire
popped your teeth   welded
your spinning head
in place

deep traveler
what prehistoric graveyards
did you see on your way
to Utopia?

what hard-bought love
did you rescue or lose
in the oil-slick
dungeons of the Earth?

                -- Hillary Lyon

The Stuntwoman Considers Ending it All

She is an adrenaline junkie.
In her third eye,
angel wings jut from scapulae.
Flying is a mindset.
What a sick twist.

The hung over crew sets up over a cliff.
Craft service has a hard time
keeping the carbs un-moist.

The male bit players wear leather,
punch and flip all over themselves.
Then, ACTION!!

She runs and hurls herself with glee
over the muscle made brigade, over the mountain,
into the water below.
Cut. Applause.

The shot goes so well this could've
been a snuff film.
What is death, after all, if not a show?

She braces against the ocean, like electricity
the waves flip on and off
over and under.

A Death Metal dirge will be added in post.
Blue black shades leap to meet her in a swirl of
comic/tragic mask choreography.

Like a competent dance partner,
the waves hold her well.
The fish open their mouths in one last "O."
the seaweed slime parts like Crispin Glover's hair.
She imagines last memories:

Her boyfriend's smoky tongue.
Chinese take-out with Lorraine.
Dress shopping for opening night.
The white tent above and behind her,
the blackness down deep, easy and forever.

They say brain waves freeze
at the exact moment of passing.
Conscious thought drifts away,
a parallel universe opens up to us all.
Or it's just gray matter synapse nonsense
devised from too much PBS watching.

The PA's are agog,
but also bored
they yearn for violence.

And what is the ocean if not even keeled?
She's not dead, just plays it that way,
likes floating "in between" for a while,
feels her black eyeliner run down pancake makeup
away from her tough, chewed up soul.

The water is an eraser.
She will live to die again tomorrow.

-- Jennifer MacBain-Stephens

Solstice

Cyclical:
      forget how
      to swallow,
fingertips
bluon particles
      exiting   a
      cavernous
      orifice
Incandescence:
electromagnetic sugar diversified
      into mason jars
Nuclear fizzle:
      heating pad
      tendons on
what mystifies all physicians—
the lower back   spines stupefy
Explosive:
      Extracted teeth
      found in the cellar
Invoke:
      enkindled
      doll skin
Revel:
mums scald
      the world
an ignited
receiving
blanket
Calcify:
      drought
      damaged
roots and toes
Steel: an
aluminum
encased
body

sweltering
palms,
like
early onset
      dementia
Char : memory,
remains burned , scattered ash
My body:
      exists to
harden,
Brain waves:
      emblaze
planets
waiting for the burn
I didn't know I wanted

-- Jennifer MacBain-Stephens

January Journal: Saturday, January 26, 2013

Late night drivers return to ice-glazed
walkways and porch steps. Air tastes garlic
raw—and cruel like exposed buried bones.
Wind blows cayenne puffs of Canada
breath. It seers eyes and scalds cheeks. Its tongue
wraps numbing knots on finger joints. It
fumbles keys. They crash down the cement
porch steps like broken china. The moon's
spotlight spots them. There they are. There's the
knob, the key slot. The door falls open.
Securely banished, the brute force of
now's dark interrogations is shut
out, while up-stream, with no earthly care,
the moon's full-face brightness orbits on.

-- Don Mager

October Journal: Friday, October 18, 2013

Lungs do not gasp for air . . . they gasp in . . .
the crisp noon Chablis of it. The cool
cider spike of it. The butterfly
tremulous flight of it as it skims
from Aster to Aster. Mum to Mum.
Imbibing the extravagance of
it, with its prick of fresh sharp menthol,
air brushes out webs from sinuses.
Its ocean spray against pores scrubs off
the tongue and washes out the throat.
Air lifts its cool noon solidity
all the way up to the lake-still sapphire
sky. Lungs of yogis draw stillness back
down through organs and breathes it back out.

-- Don Mager

Smoldering

The glowing embers
in the hearth
burned
slowly and evenly
like controlled passion:
unexplored and unspent

-- Susan Mahan

Water

A swirl of fins and bubbles,
waves and cataracts,
the falling rain,
always in motion.
Each drop, sweet elixir,
crystal hues sweeping to indigo.
Always consoling,
mermaids dream,
lulled by the crashing waves.
Capture their magic in moonlit dew.

-- Kim Malinowski

Air

Hair blowing in tornadoes
no different
than in a breeze's soft caress.
A gust, a gale,
the wind clarifies,
binds us together,
plant, animal, sky.
We breathe.
Such diversity in constant revelry,
battle of strength,
carrier of hope.

-- Kim Malinowski

Elements of Evaluation

The pageant's contestants moved on stilettos whose straps chained and constricted their feet. They spent hours eradicating blemishes, styling hair, and wearing masks made for them by other hands. Long before they felt they were ready, they marched through blinding spotlights, faces etched into cliffs of learned confidence.

Beyond the stage, the judges watched, lined up from solid to plasma, earth with a rock-hard face, water with a flowing current of hair, air with breezy motions, fire sending cinders across the table while tapping blazing fingernails. Once the contestants finished their spectacle of beauty, talent, and rhetorical skills, they marched off the stage, and the elements withdrew to a private room to deliberate.

"They all seemed a bit rigid to me," Air said.

"I thought they were rather flimsy myself," Earth countered. "But humans tend to be. What about you, Water?"

"Absolutely stunning in their own rights, but they lacked some ripple I just can't explain."

"They lacked a burning passion," Fire noted. "They weren't in their elements at all. A bunch of fish trying to swim in volcanoes."

Air nodded and murmured, "They seem very practiced to me."

"All their graces were staged," Water explained. "That's the problem with them. The ripple they lacked was natural poise."

The four elements gave a collective nod.

"Perhaps one or two of them had a spark or few…" Earth gave a low hum and looked at the other judges. "We're supposed to select a winner, you know."

"Perhaps we should pick ourselves," huffed Air.

"Nonsense. Remember what happened the last time the elements held a pageant. Discord and disaster!" Fire said, flicking a cinder towards the corner. "Part of me is loathe to admit it, but that was a delightful time in our long existence."

"But not without its drawbacks." Earth glanced to each element in turn.

"Yes, it's coming back to me now," Air replied, drifting into some distant reverie.

Water took a moment to reflect before stating, "We never did decide which of us is the most beautiful."

The words transformed the silence into something unpleasantly tight and binding. Fire and air both fidgeted. Earth, well-grounded as usual, sat with folded hands and a stern expression.

"Perhaps some things are better left to individual judgment." They all nodded at Fire's sage words, and Fire leaned back with folded arms. "Perhaps… that's the answer we give them."

The contestants, whose dazzling evening wear concealed the flaws they silently ruminated over, watched the judges pass. At center stage, Earth handed an envelope to the announcer, who said a few words to further tighten the suspense before drawing a breath. "And the winner is…" Then came the hush so complete that Air could feel the breaths of everyone in the room. Human hands ripped the envelope and withdrew a paper that was a bit wet and a bit charred and perhaps smudged with dirt. Carefully, the announcer unfolded the paper, then looked at the judges, truly looked at them, as if seeing the face of beauty for the first time.

His heart skipped a beat, and then another. And then, he fell like a stone.

Shouting erupted, followed by movement towards the door. Spectators were calling for ambulances or rushing for the exits. The contestant whose talent was first aid rushed to the rigid man, but he was beyond helping. Only the elements were unmovable. Fire flicked the curtain, and suddenly, smoke was billowing upwards. The sprinklers deposited water on the body, on the four judges, and on the dumbfounded girl with unnatural muteness. "Judge us," they commanded in unison, and the foundation trembled at their words. Fire danced a flamenco with air; Water waltzed with Earth.

The contrast in tempo between the two pairs struck the judge as quick steps and slow paired in terrifying perfection. Even as they traded partners—even after—the four of them maintained their poise and rhythm. She sat motionless, captivated by their movements and without the fear of death. Air whirled the smoke away, and when the flames neared, water washed them out and earth split the ground to collect the deluge. Finishing their performance, all four of them lined up and waited for judgment with folded hands and natural expressions.

When the firemen arrived, they found no body and no judges. Just a scorched, sodden, smudged, half-buried piece of paper whose beautiful knowledge had been lost forever.

-- Amanda M. May

East River, New York City

We pass over a river which is part of the ocean.
An ocean so vast we become mirrored in
streams of light. Over blue water fields,
we search with our faces looking downward.
Our bodies calm and liquid breathing soft saltiness.
Often we became so happy we saw the sky
as a mirror of tranquility, its brightness
coming from our heavenly ocean.

Bewildered sometimes by an ocean of life,
our faces were covered with tears. This while
this long moment seems without meaning.
Meandering back and forth in sickening motion
over and over until we could not find any
thread of thought that makes sense.
Only sorrow and vague monotony.

But most of our time was terribly rapid. Each
wave following another. One night falling faster
than the next in a wonderful swift race of days.

-- Joan McNerney

Ash Wednesday

The sky is smudged
like my forehead.

Gray clouds dump rain
then ferry snow to the mountains.

Today I fill my pen
with rainwater

and sketch invisible letters
on a naked puddle.

-- Mark J. Mitchell

Out of the Sea

In a black dory, an old woman rocks,
fishing. Her line snags on forgotten books.

A boy swims grimly, out past the gray point.
Past the surf line. Through the tide. Out of sight.

A wrecked wooden boat, threatening, starts to sway
into the channel, breaking this heedless sea.

In the hold, a dark woman cooks something.
You may taste it, but you must sing.

-- Mark J. Mitchell

Soliloquy Sacrament

Take notice: a girl
is quartering the sky,
trimming the fog,
the mist, into a
puzzle of consonants.
The mountains
laugh, become punctuated
sentences, streamlined paragraphs
etched onto the heavens
by shadows playing
like rocky inkwells.
A fox cries out in
the snow to be injected
into the text
as a question mark
of possibilities.
A cardinal fluffed against
the wind brings quilled prayers
from its feathered throat.
What
she once loved about the wilds—the harsh
cadence of its grammar
you have come to embrace:
the way

trees stark and bare
pointed limbs, exclamation marks
for the surprise
revise the wilderness wastes
into a ragged novella—
boulders, creek rocks
indirect objects posing unanswerable
questions.

Be still—this is the firmament unstitching
its holy vapors

draping you
in a sacrament of ice, sleet,
a cloud soliloquy
printing its measured text
across the hills, the sage
colored roll of land, the muddy
brambles growing like a foreign
alphabet, lambdas begging the
mute sky to speak,
to sing arias of yellow leaves,
withered days like moldering
love letters, bright berries
coloring the tree line.
You walk now in sacrament's
realm that does not know
cathedrals, place of unknowing
nature.
Thought's melody replaced
by terran strains, musical
testimony voiced in thin
streams—day's witness
to the final punctuation.

-- Ralph Monday

The Hawk's Quill

People think I am crazy when I tell them
that hawks follow me everywhere.
They fly in front of me like feathered
ICBMs when I drive, perch in trees and
gaze upon me with eyes that are like
chipped flint, savage judgment mated to
beak, talon, tender mercies only in the
plummet, the red gore of intestines sliding
in and out like wet tides pulled at by the moon.

Spirit animal whose feathers are quills writing
a thousand texts in blood, tattooed meaning
directed by a shake of feathers, a cocked head
peering like some Elizabethan king waiting to
nod to the hooded executioner for the ax to fall.
My son didn't believe me until one day he saw,
in a city parking lot, a hawk standing below the
driver's door of my truck. Waiting.
Waiting for me.
She never flew until I was five paces away.
Then, in a seedpod burst of power she was in the
sky, wings knowing the lover's air, she circled
until we drove away, followed like a hound
on a scent for miles.
The hawk is the messenger of the spirit world.
They tell me I am a tuning fork vibrated by the
cadences of seasons, hawks the equinox crossing
my equator. My son does not have the gift; suburbs
sifted the essence away, but I a thing of wild
mountains, streams, deep forests, have seen the
ghost at the top of the totem.

-- Ralph Monday

Owl Woman

I found her scented
beneath my tongue,
an old woman, not wise.
Specter of caverned hieroglyphs
shawled, tattered, her eyes
Weird almanacs that reflected
burnt out fires.
I dared not speak to a dead dream.
Her abuse nested in the tops of trees.
Peculiar perversities that she shared with
me like a dry bone.
They rattled like a *conquistadores'* sonic boom
to centuries come.
Gathered steam and rolled over me like a
Delphic vision.
I left her, roosting in a tree top,
gnawing a disemboweled animal.

-- Ralph Monday

Listen to the Ground

Do not fear this place. All is as it should be.
A mask that must be stripped away so that you see
more than the moon   boney   white   its frosted
tongue chastising this scarecrow in an empty field.
     You with your   city ways—listen, eyes turned
to smoke. Do you hear the   disturbed anguish of
cows chewing winter cud?
     Heralds are all about. The trees   turn to burgundy
wine, as someday your hair a silver aspen.
     The decay is deceiving. Taste and hear the way
you never could in those anonymous   times   in
city lights, smog-filled dreams.
     Ride this time as you would your shredded
childhood. Listen: vultures pick at a carcass in the
corn   sleeping with the roots is an underground
queendom of beetles   worms   earthbugs.
     More than autumn debris, this is a living
morality—churches   at   the end of every field,
Eucharist and the   moon making   sacrament
of crows   picking at the sienna stubble.
     Draw quietly this October   dew   dancing
with the dead.   Sap withdraws living blood to sleep
for a time   the fire in the   trees   burned   to
winter ash.
     Inhale this day. Do not fear the mask.
Staunch your wound with the living.

-- Ralph Monday

Going from Colorado

Going now, going, air empty beneath
this metal eagle winging away from
the mountains that bisect the continent
like bison splitting the Great Plains.
Though here, I remain there when the
sun is nearly burnt for the day, mountain
tops white giant knuckles of some brooding
god.
There are rivers of light up here,
thin stitched threads knitting man's
land together, weak flesh marriage
of metal coil, electrical filament,
train and engine and humming
generator that can never withstand
earth's vibrations, the roots in the
womb—the ice and religious snow
soon to come to those tethered pines
left behind.
I would crawl in among them and make
my tepee, become a primitive papoose
poised for a ripe apple plucking, listen
to the drums among the tree tops speaking
of the truths of wind, of sky, of rain,
of red-blossomed western heavens.
When the storms came from the west,
ice and snow and fury unleashed,
cathedrals poured from metal skies,
I would be nature's smith heeding
the hammered out songs of the people
long gone who knew these trails
not as dirt—life veins surging through
each untold generation's hands,
hieroglyphs marking the mirror of
undivided earth and sky.
Here the rock becomes a cradle,
the elk wise old archetypes

guiding the way by antler,
the trees holders of muted
secrets sat down before the
rock rose from earth's molten
bowels to form these solid sheets
as tin-colored tablets waiting
for each day to chisel out meaning
from sun to sun, moon to moon
in an old, old play centered
upon the center at the heart of the
galaxy.

-- Ralph Monday

Olive Trees, Alto Alentejo

Fallen into this wood, this filigree
a thousand years old, text of a time
written in atom lengths, cursive as wind,

I stand before the olive like a weed
returning without memory each May,
and front the long-lived, earth purposed

signature of the Alto Alentejo.
Signing my way, its flattened truck
of spider webs of iron wood,

more wall than colonnade, scrub high
under midsummer glint of light green leaves
on a landscape of castle towns

cut into the crowns of granite hills,
I who am the split in a second of millennium
would move so quickly as to catch fire.

The place absorbs our names.
Évoramonte of oak orchards, of fish
and wines, of the dry hills rung drier

in war, by religious ravages,
by the circular planters and strippers
of trees, from future into past amid

perpetual but annual dirt and vine,
leaving olives to bud,
everything moving into itself,

the whirl of wood signatures, map of seasons,
a history that flows in blood, by the dead,
back to the seeds of this tree.

Signposts on the Alentejo,
of Phoenicians following Romans,
following Celts, where Christian followed Muslim,

dolmen became tomb, became grave,
where the human nutrients soak into
the soil like a hand grasping its hair.

-- George Moore

Unwanted Origami

Hard nodules of cells
fold out into the world
to collapse in a breath.

No drugs she says
all this is part of the art of dying,
what we live for,

and me driving mad
across a thousand miles of desert
in the beam of a headlight

to make the last moment
of earth and air, of her fire,
that elemental essence

that evaporates into memory,
washing over this last
most ridiculous second of a life

when cells dance their wild tango
and swirl their lover toward dust
on shores of lymph and bone.

Swans in the bloodstream,
these words float on debris,
but that is the clock,

rock, stratosphere, heat,
what we live by perpetually.
Waves break us down,

waves carried to home,
folds we made in time,
mother to son.

               -- George Moore

Kola, Oblast

Pomors, seasiders,
their white sea, treeless
plain warming, sea
warming, slipping
dead first into
the 21st century, earth
sleeps, word trunks
without limbs on the
Russian seaboard.

Under foot, tundra
wakes after millennia,
whale's smallest terrain,
blind boots snowshoes,
ring on the rock.

Arctic domain, no
ecotone as treeline meets
a meager soil,
no space for birds,
no harbor for icy
human things, no retreat.
Time a supernal click of rock.

Out in truer ends
of earth, hair grass
and pearlwort reign
with a hundred lichen
and brumal mosses.

Now, the rapid repopulation,
rabbits and mice, stray cats,
crowd the frugal sub-terrain,
out of sync
in the lean biotic.

Tundra wars
below, what changes
meticulous, scanty,
a rhythm animals
themselves change?
The old pray for frost,
roots run deep
enough to survive.
What stays? But always,
it is what remains.

-- George Moore

Kingdom of Sea

Shore swells compelled by the moon,
and driven by massive currents
crest, curl and thunder down,
a process of eons, carving rock into sand,
boring a shelf into the rugged continent.

Light strewn coral beds form,
a divine circus of lively function,
where colors have fins,
where eels sway their grotesque heads,
jellies drift in, mollusks sieve the waves,
and big lipped groupers idly fan the water.
Ocean turtles stop in for rest,
fins leaning on rock over orange stars,
purple urchins, frenetic crabs.

Further out in that cobalt blue,
bullet nosed swift hunters abound,
slicing through the water,
screaming towards prey.
They shatter schools in frenzy, eat and gorge
the bloodied column now littered with flesh.

Those bits sift down,
settle in the abyss,
where meters long ribbon fish,
anglers and bizarre bioluminescent fish
reside in blackness,
where molten vents host strange worms
in the starless midnight
of the fathomless deep.

Way above, traveling cetaceans fly though
in brighter light,
gliding as whales, whacking the surface
discovering krill,

and dolphins speed by chattering,
they breech and plunge,
pirouette and dance in the volumes,
in the ancient sea, spawner of life
our salt tears a vestige of then,
a link to the water planet.

-- Heidi Morrell

Waters That Move

Listen, you may hear it
as it flows idly round the curve
by the cottonwoods, its meandering surface
glistening in the late afternoon sun.
It sounds as it washes over the stones,
gurgling and sighing its perennial
story to anyone who pauses.

Yet in the mountain highlands,
it roars and hisses, boils and foams
plummeting from snow melt
its swift velocity unstoppable,
shooting by pines, moose and
soaring raptors looking for movement
in a wild blackberry tangle.

Boulders move down gorges,
but not while you're looking,
never while you're looking.
It's when the churning mists rise up
in the spring melt, the loud erosion,
pushing pushing water, until rocks crack against rock,
when birds scatter, coyote startles.
And we, asleep in our soft bed miles away.

-- Heidi Morrell

Spine of Continents

Pushed up from earth crust movements,
or spewed from the hot belly of it's core,
created mountain ranges form a spine,
the bones of continents.
Cloaked in tree and bush
except on the highest peaks,
all yield revelation.

Spinal bones house a wonderland of life,
woven into a fortuitous web of drama
and interdependence,
predator and prey,
wolf and deer, bear and fish,
hawk and rabbit, cougar and goat.

Sapphire sky arcs over new snow melt
pounding down gorges, over precipices,
down hill sides, into rock strewn ravines,
finally easing into rivers
gradual in the flat lands.

Tension and serenity both here,
spirits in the trees,
gathered in instinctual symphony,
music of our universe.

-- Heidi Morrell

A Nicer Person than Me

You tell me
to wait for you
the same way
a person on fire
waits for water
and
a person who cannot swim
waits for someone who can –
burn
sink
then at the bottom
with darkness for skin,
wait for someone else

-- Kacper Niburski

Fossil Fuel

You're extinct
even though
you're only eight
and you're helping
to turn on the stove
as a dinosaur roars
to cook the chicken dinner,
which is a failed dinosaur,
which you are too -
and also a failed bird -
until you a bit of both
joining the
boned and the boneless
in a meteoric rise of food and fingers
of a lover or enemy
depending on how hard
you close your hand
or how open you can make it,
that one day crashes into the ground
leaving a six feet hole
wide open
then closed
without your hands
and the world is swallowed
for dinner
like a dinosaur's chomp

-- Kacper Niburski

The Patron Saint

Santa Ana is the patron saint of cabinet makers,
horseback riders,
and unmarried mothers.
She becomes the patron saint of the insane
when her hot breath sweeps over Los Angeles.

The devil winds are rattling
the window panes of my soul.
They prickle my skin,
sending bolts of fire up my nose.
I am sneezing and itching,
my gums swelling like pink pillows.

As I walk the dogs at dawn,
dust swirls up the street searching out victims.
Wildfires blaze in the hills,
adding embers to
the Santa Ana cocktail—
bits of trees and homes,
plastic crumbs
and treasured documents,
are inhaled.

On a white wall
someone wrote in pencil:
Please Kill Me!
Walking further,
I see a new man living
near the onramp to the freeway.
He is wearing rags and living
in a pile of useless trash and chaos.
Yet on top of this mess,
is a clean wooden salad bowl
with two clean salad servers
crossed in the bowl like praying hands.

I can smell the sadness
on the stained fingers of the wind.

-- Suzanne O'Connell

Song of the Sea Wanderer's Wife

Tonight, my pleasure of
Lost on edges of slant rain

Lightening rules sky
through heavy storms .

Wet drops sizzle.
on the hearth

He is not here.
No one weaves the rushes.

Bone dust and bog heave up
Days lost, years pass

ancient ghosts I cannot see.
crash onto the white sands.

curls round the sweet moon
After storm I walk the night

We have lost each other
I hold my strength
lurching home
to the clasped safety

clouds forsaken.
dark, cold, and hard.

west winds crash
I hide new scars on hands and face.

My cat mews and crawls inside
throughout the house.

He is not home
No one to thatch the roof.

bronzed tips of broken swords
once sinless they flee towards

Desperate I cry salt tears. Salt waves
Smoke rises through the dirt floored cottage,

so full and low in the sky.
vanquished beach which waits with me.

our eyes, our once red hair
lost, for scarecrow men
away from war
of memory mist Clew Bay.

-- Mary C. O'Malley

Chambers Creek

gliding parallel in tandem
young mallard and his mate
eyes wide laughing loud

arrive in sliding splashes
noisily shake off excitement
wake once slumbered silence

waves encircle widen wane
diminish to prior smoothness
before reaching shore where

poised at water's edge a lone
blue heron like the vigilant
school librarian keeps watch

-- Carl Palmer

You tell this ice the glass
is breaking up, to take
one breath more :a splash

starting out, half as shoreline
the other frozen underneath
so you don't drown the way each shadow

still has the scent from seawater
though the frost
is already holding your hand

face down, deeper and deeper
in pieces not yet apart
--you yell breathe in, let its cold

wash over you, in you, become
water again, a mouth again
and against your lips, alone.

-- Simon Perchik

So Fleetingly

Stars are born in the great still lake below.
Above, satellites falter in their uneasy orbits.
In forward years, you'll find your lost father
waiting beyond the Perseids.

You'll remember him saying
I won't let go until you ask me to—
and even when you said it was time he never
let you see him as anything but unperturbed.

You'll live past a billion blinks of an eye,
he'd say, if you understand what it is
you're looking for. A slight breeze robs
the universe of stars.

They were never as real as the water that
held them, however so fleetingly.

-- Richard King Perkins II

Water in Louisiana

As ever, it begins with the eyes.
A glowing in darkness
which isn't the moon-opus of tonight
but dissolves into an effluvium
hiding in streams of Spanish moss.

Water confirms our concept of justice—
too much, we drown,
too little, we wither.
It is your rippling that awakens clouds
to give up the heaviness of their mélange.

A magenta river strolls languidly
through a glade of cypress trees—
water challenges our concept of justice;
like the child who suffocates in an inch of liquid
or the sailor who dehydrates
in a seascape of saline oceans.

The nest wedged between barn boards
exists in partial shelter,
a compound fracture
partially exposed to cloudbursts—
still there is no reason to leave.
Runoff and ill intent can find us anywhere and
every thought remains an evening prayer for Louisiana.

The fertile delta deposits form a lush triangular islet—
your shy vital secret
kept behind nervous giggles
and beneath the belly's swell.

Eyes closed now, our kiss begins at the end
of the river's mouth.

I never knew your name, cherie—

but remember your sanctum sanctorum
in my most private vespers
saved for waters
we once nightly traveled.

-- Richard King Perkins II

My Fire at Dawn

Across lolling brackish water, fire-tendrils skitter,
lurking clouds impaled—
and possibly, the sky-ember conscripts my mind.

Uncertain aspect of daybreak wends and pries
through a brindled pasture

to worry at branch tips, sledge at fence posts

unslumbering the matchless silicone lying above,
exposing a singular fascination—

a chestnut pony my daughter
once rode shakily at a party.

Sunlight tongues an invitation to its deepest tissue;
an imperious beckoning and unjust congruence
threatened only by meeting
the dark of yesterday.

Dawn outstrips any fond notion of morning—
chapped, abraded;
I lie exposed in a gulf of fields.

I will be viewed later,
desolate flake falling to a point above the horizon,
wind-fins retracted, trajectory zero.

Sunlight must forever pursue itself
bringing the dual-edged gift of heat—

the harsh reveal of morning,
forcing the earth to spin involuntarily,

waiting for my fire to catch.

-- Richard King Perkins II

Elemental Haiku

I am the land and
the land is me, I feel the
earth beneath my feet.

I taste water in
the air, feel it seep beneath
my skin; nourishing.

I breath the mist that
lingers long; inhale the breeze
that dances through leaves.

I feel fire within
my soul, passionate, deadly
exploding power.

-- Freya Pickard

Corrections and Clarifications

It was nothing more than sloppy journalism. He had noticed it, not only because of his expertise in the subject, but also because he'd read the official report on the incident. Now, one ill-researched fact had swept away the identity of her short life, cementing her legacy as *the girl who was killed by the undertow*.

This is the process: wind pushes the water to the shore; water streams along the shoreline, until it finds an exit route back to its source; water returns to the sea at an average speed of 1.5m per second, taking along with it souvenirs from the beach. Technically this is known as a rip current; an occurrence far more dangerous than the undertow. There are few warnings: sometimes the water changes hue, to a murky brown, as sediment is ripped from the sea bed, or maybe there is a parting of the breaking waves.

After he wrote to the newspaper, they rectified their mistake. A one-liner was printed below Thursday's TV picks, headlined in a small bold font: *Corrections and Clarifications*.

Some weeks later, the local council placed a notice where the beach narrowed and passed into the cove. It reminded him of the dying flowers that often mark the site of a road death. It read: DANGER, STRONG UNDERTOW. He wrote to the town hall, pointing out their mistake. Their reply thanked him and assured him the matter would be raised at the next general meeting.

Each morning, he stands on the cliff's edge, looking down to where his replacement sits on her chair, high above the summer bathers. He contemplates the little mistakes people make, such as not knowing the difference between a rip current and the undertow; or not noticing a child, her curly ginger hair washed across her face like a sea creature's sprawling tendrils; the flailing arms, greased with factor 40; cries for help muted by breakers and mouthfuls of the salty sea; thrown about like a cork, at the mercy of the surf, moving rapidly away from land.

He watches the water for a sign. Any sign.

-- Tim Roberts

Keep Still While Storms Flatten Mountains

-- after Stonehouse or Shiwu, a Chinese Chan poet and hermit, 1272-1352

you run away with me as far as the sea
we sink, pummeled by pale grey crested waves
in the pale grey sea, churned with sand
we are rubbed smooth by sand as fine as talc
as sticky as semen and the smell of sea

occasionally we run aground
the waves clap like hands above our heads
our hands wave like waves above the sea
we chase the sweet souls of the drowned
in the sticky sound of dreams

the push and thrust
the gentle melody understands
the rhythms of attention
a face turned to the light
and a seagull wheeling overhead—

a flock of black parentheses
skim the cobalt sea
wheel and dip, heading west
wingtips curved in honor
of *the hues of blue* (one day I'll write

yesterday the air was filled with light and colour
today dense clouds hover over the rocky shore
the wind scrapes softly, then with such ferocity
in our treehouse we are tossed as if we were at sea
at the mercy of the waves

I take up blind writing to hold the waves
the braying of the hounds at bay
on my way home, a fox crosses my path

the waves knock me off my feet with a laugh
I laugh and shed sea spray like jewels

-- Francesca Sasnaitis

Valéry on the Beach

Summer's first hot day knocks me flat—I read Valéry on the beach,
Man and Seashell, appropriate no? The brim of my straw hat
emulates the mantle of a broken bivalve,

lilts in rhythm with the sun's barbed sparks riffling off the sea.
Behind tangerine shades, round as a flathead's drowning mouth,
my eyes skid across the impenetrable blue,

gulp at the limits of sky, the wedge of land, the white horizon,
ogle the interstice between the naked and the clad
spread-eagle on the shore. The life on land's too hot,

the sun's made coals of sand. I dive across the glare expanse
and down—steam rises from water's blessed contact, where I
search for treasure, the gleam of the divine in the dappled green,

but find only fool's gold, a rusty mollusc thick with age,
the old man of seashells, grown ridged and ringed
as ancient jarrah, his calcareous body convoluted

by processes mysterious to human minds, and perfect,
in its way more perfect than my manmade hat,
designed and reproduced for mass consumption.

I break the surface, breathe, and turn face down to search
the sun stippled depths. Stones and shells gleam below
but lose their lustre as soon as they're exposed,

underwater art undermined by air and light.
The opal abalone fades to dull metallic sheen;
the elegant pheasant shell is stripped of ink.

I will throw back this shell I've found, this singular shell,
representative of the boundary between below and above,
this distraction from the flow. To paraphrase Valéry,

this seashell has served me well, reminding me
of nature's art, alien organic activity, my dislocated body,
what I am or might be, what I know, and don't.

-- Francesca Sasnaitis

hail lashes windows
jolts me from my noontime nap
fearing tornado

-- Emily Jo Scalzo

The Elements of Palling Around

We were a crescent around the fire
A human Ottoman flag
With camp chairs' legs submerging into the Earth
Probing for a home
As we searched for meaning
In shots of fire water clouded by crushed up
Opiates and muscle relaxants and benzodiazepines
And finding that significance
In friendship
Laughter
And the song of cicadas that filled the summer air

-- Keenan Schott

Elemental

> *-- a belief in classical and medieval times that everything on earth, including mankind, was composed of the four elements.*

We are water without a cup,
not to be lifted or poured;
cataract contracting darkness,
solution of word.

We are flames without a hearth,
fire's bedrock of sense
having heart's eyes for sun's shine
liquid in lens.

We are earth without a world,
slightly soured rich ground
warm while acres' sufficiency
crumbles in hand.

We are air within the context
of conditional breath:
creation confused by confine,
elements of myth.

-- Belinda Singleton

A Hundred Paper Rivers

on an overly sunny day
along a pock-marked sidewalk
the keen-eyed walker
found a long suicide note
better to call it a letter
all ten pages
in a printed hand
neat as discarded memory
the signature smudged
so even under a magnifying glass
it was problematic at best

the keen-eyed walker
rips the ten-page letter
into a hundred paper rivers
going to the darkness of the world
and tosses river after river
into the dumfounded air
fearing disorder and messiness
would mean disqualification
from salvation or redemption
then rips the last page
again and again
so God wouldn't be able
to read a single word

-- J.J. Steinfeld

Pulling Up the Light

long line of geese, ragged wave in a row faintly rising and falling
and rising, one bird slightly ahead, the rest ranging a little behind
all flapping hard, calling and honking as one flock appear
at dawn headed north above flowering pink trees
they pull sunrise up after them, yellow and pink
over the far plateau, they pull the light with them
waving in their wavering line drawn across the pale sky

-- Emily Strauss

Amelia Earhart Flies at Night

I tried to imagine this darkness. I tried
to prepare: dove into the lake, my breath
a curtain against light. I touched bottom,
clawed my way through mud. But the curtain
split, let in the sun and I rose to it. That dark

was nothing like this. Water below, and I
hurtle headlong through air, though I can't
tell one from the other: not water from sky
nor earth from water. No tracks but mine—
tracks I can't follow—behind me. It's not

that I'm small, I and this contraption I ride.
It's that darkness is so big. Here, I nudge
a mere stick and my great wings respond,
as if I control the forces that control them.
Yet I know the truth: I fly on a whim of air

over a treachery of sea. What do mariners
think of as they sail through night, waves
calm enough, wind obliging? Do they dare
ponder the liquid dark? If the lost ones
could speak, I wonder what they'd say,

the ribs of their ships stripped as bare
as their own. When you fly, you're not
man or woman, not human or flesh, just
a bundle of matter moving through
nothing. Sea. Wind. Earth. Sky. Words

for the same thing: for what I think
I ride. Though I pretend otherwise,
here, in the dark, I edge a little closer

to what rides me—up here, where
the heavens open, where the hells open.

-- Linda Strever

Ebb Tide at Woodard Bay

A heron stands on one leg, motionless, wings spread
to warm in waning sun. Tide low to mud flats,

brown, the opposite of parched: wet, slippery, full
of tiny life. Refusal might not mean what you think—

just grass leaning toward the bay in wind, no choice
but to bend as the heron bends in its swift piercing

of fish, its fast swallow, its reflection on the slick,
shining mud, the smell of decay, of rich leavings,

of comings and goings, recedings and reachings.
The same wind ruffles feathers, lifts the bird's wings

as it rises full-bellied into bluegreen sky. If you
could ride its dark back into the coming night,

you would know. You'd settle into the high nest,
feathers a weightless protection against cold.

-- Linda Strever

The Library of Air

-- Inspired by Roni Horn's Library of Water

Where is the library of air, she asks,
turning to the library's
enormous windows
and the brilliant sun, the clarity
that heightens each blade of grass,
each grain of sand.

She remembers
her grandparents' never-opened
can of New Hampshire air.
She remembers
rolling down the car window
to breathe in Maine
and getting a lungful of exhaust
instead.

She imagines being a visitor
from the Chinese city of Harbin
traveling to the library of air,
looking for the column of
orange and brown cloud,
its sulfur contained by glass,
which is her air, and finding
these transparent columns,
these words not in her language,
these pockets of air
that someone else, some
English-speaker, some
Icelandic-speaker
can breathe.

-- Marianne Szlyk

At The Library of Water

-- After Roni Horn's permanent installation

Cloudy white, beige, and yellow
columns occupy this open hall,
so much unlike the dark, untidy stacks
of a library of books.
Not solid like marble,
these columns let light shine through.
In even rows, they take up space
that books and study carrels would.

The only words in this library
materialize on the floor,
the way great men's names and faces
once did: Shakespeare, Dante,
Vergil, Ovid, Homer, and so on.
These words in Icelandic and English
indicate weather phenomena,
something less personal
than a man who lived and died
or his footnoted works that one reads in
dog-eared, highlighted paperback.
But all of us, even the common woman,
the common reader,
even Samuel Johnson,
experience the weather.

Still she wonders what a Californian,
a refugee from burnt hills and dry wells,
would make of this library,
the columns of what her state is missing,
a luxury fetish like caviar
or extreme thinness
in the era of cheesy fries,
corn syrup, and unlimited soda pop.

And what would a Floridian--
someone whose city is melting,
dissolving in brown water--
make of these columns
prizing water as if it were scarce,
as if it weren't drowning
his city, his street, his home.

-- Marianne Szlyk

Nighttime Accomplice

A passing boat caused a wake in the 'no wake' area. Grabbing a rail to steady his already unsteady legs, Mac Ellis lurched sideways on the dock, fell heavily and hit his head on the third of six steps that led down to where the old yacht Stella By Night rode deep in her berth. The boat lines snapped and struggled against the unexpected swells and blended with the night sounds of Shoreside Marina.

74 years old and running on a gallon of midnight adrenalin and a bottle of cheap vodka, he stumbled down the dock toward Slip 8 grasping pylons with shaky hands, unaware of the amber eyes that stared from a hidden cave of underbrush on the shore, unaware of the curious gaze that watched his every move.

Alone, Mac spent his days on a park bench watching the ocean or at the homeless camp down in the grove, his nights were spent cocooned in the humid musty innards of old Stella's tarped dinghy. Like him, the boat had seen better days and he didn't think she'd mind a homeless stowaway. It was 11 o'clock before he wormed his way under the heavy cover and took refuge in darkness and a fitful sleep.

An hour later he woke to the vibrations of the yacht's engines. *Who are those people? Why the hushed voices?* He had watched the yacht for weeks before deciding to make himself at home, no one had come near the old vessel. *Why now?* He heard the lines and bumpers being cast off and footsteps came close to the dinghy. *What was that thump? What did they throw on board?* He tried to be invisible in the midnight shadows, laying motionless he held his breath and wished he could silence his heartbeat. Someone mentioned a bay in Catalina. *Who are these men?* Stella By Night left the harbor and lulled by the vodka and the dinghy's sway, Mac rolled into a fetal position, head cradled on a life jacket.

. . . Raindrops splattered the dock and hydrated a thick stain of dried blood to a pale red liquid. The amber eyed feral cat left her underbrush cave and snuck onto the dock in search of wharf rats that inhabited the night. Creeping down toward Slip 8 she stopped to lick the sticky

sweet liquid dry with her sandpaper tongue. Lapping the spot clean, she slowly retreated to the safety of her shoreline den.

Mac Ellis woke to rain dripping through a hole in the tarp and rubbed his arms and legs to stop the thousands of needles that pricked his skin, every bone in his body ached, his head throbbed. Finding a torn grommet he looked out at the harbor lights. The yacht was safely at the dock. *Had it been a dream? Who were those voices? What about Catalina?* Noticing the cat, he watched her disappear in the shadows. Tomorrow, he decided, he'd share his can of Beenie Weenies with her.

A boat passed causing a wake in the 'no wake' area, boat lines struggled against the swells and blended with sound of the squeaking dock. Again Mac looked through the grommet hole and searched the harbor. *What am I looking for? Who were those men and what was that splash?*

In her hideout, the amber eyed cat licked a sweet taste from her bony paws . . .

-- Barbara Tate

The Masons

ex caligine lux

I. Canterbury

Another tourist, I climb the pilgrim's steps,
Curiously shamed by the mute ecstasies of God,
Of the masons. Do the faithless have martyrs?
A stone marks Becket's murder on a Tuesday.
I think, cynically, he could have locked the door.
His body, cut ear to ear, lay in the crypt
Still wearing the hair shirt of a pauper.
His brain oozed new symbols on the pavement.
Above a dozen gibbering languages,
Bell Harry tolls a faith of centuries.
A barefoot king, I pay my penny's penance,
Reflecting on this rich earth beneath heaven's lantern.
Freemasons, grotesque and smiling,
Stare down from their permanent heights.

II. York Minster

Fixed pendants, the ancient windows rise
Before me in a wall of light, raw color
Teaching the pieced magic of scripture.
Overwhelmed, I stare through Genesis and Revelation.
Christ hangs crucified in glass,
His wounds a glazed mosaic of pain.
Haloed by saints, the frail icon
Spans the elegant simplicity of stone.
Does a wall keep faith in? Outside the Minster,
A wall sleeps like a coiled serpent.
Encircling the city, its battlements
Besiege time in a war of silence.
Walking the parapet at vespers, they seem as one,
This stone necklace with its gothic jewel.

III. Saint Paul's

Heart of empire, the scarred dome of Saint Paul's
Rides like a man-of-war beside the Thames.
Hard to think of Nelson bleeding aboard Victory
In this white stillness, his legs buckling
On the quarterdeck as the sniper's bullet
Cut through his chest. Dead at four thirty,
His body drew a shroud over England,
His soul enshrined beneath the grateful entablature of myth.
Do we worship warrior or savior? Muttering aloud,
My contradictions embarrass the tomb.
Patient as history, the great admiral listens
From a stone vessel becalmed in the human sea.
Stone fades. Hands fail. What endures is duty,
A silhouette in the blitz, stubbornness.

IV. Coventry

Standing alone in the ruins, I can hear
The first incendiaries screaming through the nave,
Mocking the credo with a rhetoric of fire.
The altar explodes, indiscriminate steel
Shattering the brilliant latticeworks.
The roof melts into white heat, forged to ashes.
Charred masons, crawling through dawn,
Gather God's agony in a metaphor of stone.
Time does not heal but adds. The new cathedral
Grows like an arm on scorched flesh.
Purified, its ministries inflame the world.
Translucent figures, weaving tapestries in glass,
Beckon the passionate industry of faith.
The cross hangs straight as a plumb-line.

-- Peter Taylor

Love Letter No. 4: To the Nail Biter

You will remember again
lying on a dry sunny beach
warm skin against rested bones.
This swim is not endless—
these swells you fight,
this constant coughing up water
will eventually subside.
Even the bleeding
edges of your cuticles
deserve your tenderness.
Because his hands will never
work that soothing magic again,
you must hold them away
from the sharpness of your teeth,
purse your lips,
and tell them they are as worthy
of your protection as your breasts,
as your pit-bull heart. As all of you
is worthy, so is the clear line
of your fingernails curving.
Cut them clean.
Even you, Olympic-storm swimmer,
can drag yourself up
on some long shore, wash salt
from your skin, hold your hands up
to the sun and say it.
Say even your cuticles are worthy
of being loved.

-- Sarah Thursday

Oceans Once Receded

I was a desert woman
who learned to live on cactus boys
learned to run at night and sleep all day
knowing the burn of sky and sand

Then you came with your oceans,
rivers, lakes, and waterfalls
I dove in, eyes closed
hoping you'd teach me to swim
hoping to learn your whale songs

I threw away my land shoes
swam under the stars
let my skin pucker in your waves
my desert plants were drowning
I let them bloat and drift away

Then your tsunami receded
first sudden, then steady and slow
I stood naked in your mud bed
for weeks with dripping hair,
dripping hands refused to dry

I learned to pray to wet earth
give thanks for saltwater baths
learned to hear your voice
in the night bird songs

Until even the mud left
took its soft clay from between my toes
the caked earth in my hair
began to dry and crumble
desert wind wiped all traces
of salt from my cheeks

I push myself back into desert shade
live in the evening light
I can never return to cactus fruit
when I've fed on fields of phytoplankton
I've lost the taste for prickly boys
so I may wither for a while

Until at the edge of some moment
in the pale space between sun and moon
I might hear the sound
      of water rushing

-- Sarah Thursday

My Curiosity is a Frigate

My curiosity is a frigate
heavily loaded with perishable cargo--
One day, I'm fascinated by harvester ants
and think I could study them forever,
maybe even give my life over like Dian Fossey
studying mountain gorillas, but how was butter
made three thousand years ago? Then goat butter,
yak butter, yak breeds, yak meat, yak history, yak tea--
when my interest is high-jacked by a pirate ship
throwing bundles of butter and knowledge
overboard. Gone. No resuscitating them.
My empty ship starts reloading in safe harbor
with biographies – Gandhi, Dieter Dengler,
Albert Schweitzer, Clara Schumann. I'm listening
to one of Clara's songs when strong gales
blow my frigate off course to an island.
Treasure Island, Robinson Crusoe, the indigenous
arts of the Hawaiian Islands, the fearless-eyed Israel
Kamakawiwoʻole singing *What a Wonderful World*
and *Somewhere Over the Rainbow*. Ukuleles! For a day,
I believe I'll take uke lessons or make my own stringed
instrument with a tin oil can and goat gut. Yum, goat
brochettes. But inventors are awesome. Ben Franklin's
lightning rods, swim fins. The woman Frances Wolle who
created the machine to make paper bags in 1852. Paper vs
plastic. The island of plastic bags in the ocean. My ship is taking
on water in the high seas—water microbes, water rights,
Lake Superior, fresh water, salt water, saline, salad,
Salado, salami, salsa, desalination, Salt River. Salvation –
life jackets used to be made of cork from cork trees,
as for wine bottles afloat in this, my wine-dark sea.

-- *Jari Thymian*

Looking at Phainopepla

fifty-ninth birthday
my first phainopepla
shining shadow

mesquite fire
red eyes rise
into valley dusk

white wing stripes in flight
the kachina clown flutters
on high mistletoe

tonight's new moon
shows a red dwarf star
robed in black

dark crest
my mind fruited
in the hackberry bush

-- Jari Thymian

Like a Shift Leader in a Gold Mine

Just let your thoughts leap, I thought,
and sat with pen in hand. Nothing.
Just let your mind flow, said I,
but the river was dammed. Just let
ideas reflect then jot them down,
but my mind was an empty, dull hall.
So I went to bed. The subconscious
took command like a shift leader
in a gold mine and drilled, gouged,
and sifted the deep, redolent earth.
In the morning with my mug of tea
I sat to write and discovered
a vein of luminous gold exposed
with each stroke of my pen.

-- Dennis Trujillo

Sea Otters

Sea otters hold hands while they're sleeping
so they don't drift away from each other;

lying on their backs, they float through night
like kayaks rafted together by tow ropes

lulled by the cradling rock of waves that roll
from flat to round to pointy peaks of foam

and I think that's what I miss the most.
Lying on my back with you dozing beside me

your hand draped over my heart like a gentle tent
my fingers laced through yours in a sort of truce

because when we slept no one had to be right.

-- Susan Vespoli

Unbalancing

-- inspired by Hippocrates' theory of the Four Humors, which links health and well-being to the elements.

Today, there is bile in the throat
of black winter, spitting down
on us, warm in our beds, setting
the mood as the alarm cackles
us awake before dawn.

We bleed out of the duvet, the leech
of morning sucking life
from skin. The mirror shows
no color in our cheeks.

The weight of day lunges,
its constant cough of tasks
settling in the base of our lungs,
unbalancing the spine of the clock.

We wait, need to believe
in Summer, hot blood
through veins; believe
that below our feet
a kiln will fire.

-- Claire Walker

Flood

The library's artificial air is a clumsy monkey.
Its cool hands slip away from the hem of my ankle-pants
as I walk into the afternoon, play a game of chicken
with the humidity speeding towards my face.
I retreat into the cave of my car
where the aroma of leftover fusty pizza sits on the floor.

The lyrics of *Sincerely* are still rolling off my tongue
as I pull in the driveway and gather up the frayed
end of a grocery bag filled with four audio books.
I walk inside my home with words compressed in plastic.

Above the roof, charcoal clouds apron the sky
and outside my window, a festival of colors—
geraniums with flirtatious red smiles,
begonias with pursed pink painted lips,
sunflowers with dribbling yellow hair,
and purple fingered morning glories
crawling through twines of green.

I toss the bag on the couch, humming *Sincerely,*
as water gushes out of the darkened clouds
as though Moses just lifted his rod and struck the rock.

-- Loretta Diane Walker

Falling into Morning

"The autumn wind is a villain big and bold."

-- Steve Sabol

It's evident the wind's descending into madness.
Its psychosis of shaking manifest
in scalped maples and oaks.

A lone leaf of white paper flies
towards shelter in a field overgrown with tumbleweeds.
An empty green bean can rolls until it finds refuge
underneath a parked car.

There is grief for those wind-chimes
tethered helplessly to a rusted hook;
their glassy teeth chatter fearful melodies.

But the trees are most frightened,
are too traumatized to stop shaking.
Their trembling limbs incessantly thrash against air,
leaves fall into morning.

Is it mad to say there is beauty in the wind's insanity?
The way it forces the day to press its shivering hands
against window screens?

Or the way it drags fallen leaves to a far corner
of the yard, sandwich them between concrete and sky,
their scarlet-orange bodies heaped into a chilly flame?

-- Loretta Diane Walker

A Look is the Fire Itself

Smoke fills the living room:
the couch, the chair only
shadows. She stands
patiently in the center, sees
fire lick the tips of her shoes,
jump to her skirt. She raises
arms above her head. It climbs
her arms, leaps to her hair.
When the fire department
arrives all they find
are ashes and
ghosts fleeing
through the back yard.

-- Connie K Walle

Spanish leather

We covered
mountains like storms,
rode through meadow and forest
to drink at alpine springs;
fire of ice.

We flowed with the river
green into deserts
where mirages snake-undulate
horizons; fire of earth.

We colonized the darkness
and blazed all night like stars;
fire of air,

but time wore out my boots, love,
my special, double-lined,
hand-stitched from finest
Spanish leather

that fit the way you used to -

without them, I can't ride.

-- Mercedes Webb-Pullman

Ruapehu

A cap of ice covers
the volcano,
fire always seeking
release.

Uneasily you feel
subterranean shifts,
low groans
as Ruamoko stirs.

Unborn trickster,
air of fire,
liquid earth,
he's ready to turn over
and change
the world.

                -- Mercedes Webb-Pullman

Author's Note: Ruapehu - One of NZ's active volcanos
                     Ruamoko - Maori god of earthquakes and volcanos

Ghost Dancing

My endless winter
followed our eternal summer

Our folly
the biting blue wind

hoar-frost
on my cheeks and eye-lashes

this chill air
dances as we once did

whispers, while I freeze
there is no one left who knows . . .

Who knows to dance
like the cosmic moths in the harvest moon light
(yet to fire we go also)

Who knows to dance
like the otters playful roll at sea
neverminding of the cruelty lurking beneath

Who knows to dance
upon the graves of ancestors
in praise of all that is

Who knows to dance
in the hum of knowing crowds, like fallen wasps;
the dance of forgetting

Who knows to dance
enjoy the dirt
the earthworms that consume us
the seasons carrying us to them

Like the likeness of a tree's joyous shadow
enchanting us to speak in tongues
the flipping of eyelids
cross-currents of dreams

Freezing and falling
asleep and screaming
at the nothingness,
of the nothingness, no less . . .

Ah, Sister Wind. You want your confession:
I know nothing—
but accept the cold for what you meant it to be

so unlikely a thing to be a spark
yet it feels hot

while the ghost dancers coolly approach
knowing I am theirs, and as ever

was never yours.

-- J.R. West

Incompatible

Like fire and ice
Which is softer?
    No mystic would tell you
    What signs to follow.
While Penny painted and Art
Carried a lunchpail to work, incompatible.

Like porcelain chimes in the wind
Chords made to shatter.
    Our words striking the nervous air
    Not soft sonnets, but bee stings.
Only once then gone
Friendship, incompatible.

Like field mice and soldiers
Hunger licking the razor moon.
    For us, eternity was sudden
    Its piercing claws familiar.
Traces left along the forest floor
Warning to all that still exist, incompatible.

Like the space between atoms
Relentless as a circle.
    Your silence suspending
    Years like dust in the void.
We broke something like a theory
Perfect, incompatible.

                    -- J.R. West

Angelfish

I always knew I was a fish,
my birth perched on the edge
of Pisces, water soothing me
with its cool enveloping embrace.
Sometimes I dive down deep
just to see the lemon yellow kelp,
the pink coral like pincers, the brain
coral infusing me with memories
of past loves. I'd choose to be an angelfish,
not a grey fish. I'd draw a crowd
with my blues more dazzling than the skies,
without a hint of white. I'd parade back
and forth in my splendid colors, never
stopping to think about the bones
in my belly, and I'd hear no sound of bells
or music, just the silence of the seas
and other fish rushing past.

-- Mary L. Westcott

Ode to Blue Spirit Retreat Center, Costa Rica

I float on salty water
that encircles me in the infinity
pool at the top of the hill. I gaze
at black rocks stretching ragged
to an inviting sea in a cove
of safety among the crags
and sand of a deserted beach.
Before sunset, I walk down the pathway
to the ocean. Green surpasses blue
as the color of ferns and lichen,
while purple orchids and hibiscus
dot the rocky slope. Butterflies,
yellow and brown, decorate the brush.
Magpies and hummingbirds chatter
in the surrounding trees. As the sun sets,
the branches of the Guanacaste tree reach up
to snag the stars, and the moon glows over
the dense rain forest.

-- Mary L. Westcott

At the Party Tonight

the baby is more interested
in the weather than the people
under a canopy, hiding from rain.

Arms tired from bouncing
I leave him to his father
to wander across the wet yard

to a creek in the back
full as if no one told it
rain comes to an end.

I return, party shoes
sinking in the grass
a pale moon moves

in my direction. It's growing
dark. I don't know
if he can see this far

but I smile.
A shadow-smile echo
spreads over his face

like a sudden downpour
cool and welcome
on a hot summer night

and I am drenched
and full
as if I have lived
my whole life for this.

-- Shannon Connor Winward

Remembrance

When you are gone
I will learn to speak to you
with rosemary.

Every time I kneel before the shrub
your mother gave me
I will think of you.

Every time I worry the soil
I will knead your name
every resentment I will tuck

like a secret
under the roots
where he will never think to look

With every branch pinched back
crushed and oiled in my palm
this rosemary will be your surrogate.

When you leave, this sacrifice
of friendship for love
will whisper of itself

to the back of my hand.
We used to talk like this—
remember?

-- Shannon Connor Winward

Maybe the Kindling Brings it on Herself

The spark consumes
to the quick without remorse
—better than waiting to burn.

-- Shannon Connor Winward

Where Weighty Glaciers Recede

isostatic rebound occurs—
terrain rising an inch a year.
Fresh earth emerging along shores.
New life taking root,

natural succession a lesson
not to be missed. Massive Mendenhall
Glacier just the iceberg's tip.
Blue ice split from the glacier's face—

chunks that drift like weighty lace.
But let's go back seven million years:
first small glaciers forming in those
upper elevation watersheds,

transforming V-shaped river valleys
into Us—sharpening, steepening
the ridges' crests, what ice does best.
Earth's climate chilling (more snow falling,

less melting), glaciers extending into lowlands,
coalescing to form deeper ice masses,
etching cliffs into valley walls. Frozen
tide rising, only highest peaks exposed.

Then the climate's milder mode,
ice retreating. Dozens of times,
valley and alpine glaciation. Go back
twenty-five thousand years,

ice extending west of Misty Fiords
cross-continent to Cape Cod.
Go back, fifteen thousand years
the great ice sheet beginning to retreat,

sea levels rising to flood fiords.
Back, ten thousand years, spruce and
hemlocks replacing alder, willow,
tundra vegetation. Six thousand

years, another glacial advance.
Three thousand six hundred years,
Little Ice Age was all the rage
18th to 19th century, scouring and sweeping

away like Judgment Day. Praise
glaciers and fresh earth, blue ice and
ice sheets' retreats, spruce and hemlocks
whose longevity is to be envied.

So much change and adaptability.
Blessed be the rising of terrain,
the infinite falling of snow and rain.
Natural succession made precious

by its fleeting nature. If glaciers
never moved—were as fixed as
rooted trees—would we esteem them
as much as gems?

-- Diana Woodcock

Waiting for Rain During the Drought

The ice plant is dying.
Tuesday is no water day.
The sky grays.
Angels roll their barrels.
Lightning cracks to the north.
Cat snores through thunder.
Doves abandon feeders, huddle in pine.
Message machine plays an ancient greeting.
The caller hangs up.
Asphalt waits to release smells.
Pray for umbrellas.

-- Kirby Wright

Li Na (李娜) Sonnet

Her name in green on her shoulder
left leg bent over righteous one
like hairs cover the sleeping face
protecting against sun bugs flies

She sleeps in profile on stones
to the beach where the people are
sunbathing and snorkeling and
remains fossil like herstory

When Chinese could already write
but not yet scuba dive and surf
and it's the latter what all East
and West are looking for just now

And her slippers are loosely lost next to her head
are there to remind life is not just in our dreams.

-- Xanadu

Brocken, Helm Crag

I'd zigzagged up Helm Crag,
emerging from mist into sun
just as I gained the ridge.
South-west, Harrison Stickle,
a crocodile's snout and eyes,
protruded above dazzling cloud;
across Dunmail Raise, the tawny
tops of Fairfield and Great Rigg.

Down-sun, my shadow stretched
across the dissipating mist,
its legs impossibly long,
an ephemeral glory encircling
its head. Only if you're blest
with this coincidence of earth, air,
water and fire can you see
yourself as a giant,
                         or as a saint.

-- Mantz Yorke

Fire

your soft power bursting from your ribcage
as enthusiastic as a phoenix is supposed to be
when you fly your lipless kisses
you reach out your hands
          until they are all broken

                  -- *Changming Yuan*

Wood

rings in rings have been opened or broken
like echoes that roll from home to home
each containing fragments of green
trying to tell their tales
        from the forest's depths

-- Changming Yuan

From The Editors

My Brain is on Fire

A four-alarm forest
of productivity, rising at dawn.
I cannot keep up
with full-scale thoughts, a blaze
of motivation and creativity.
The smoke pouring from my ears
is blinding. I do not know which way
to turn. I start cleaning, organizing,
only to be flooded by bombardment
of watery lines. I pour them
onto paper, try to focus their force.
It's no use. Soon I am trying to run errands,
but nothing is being
accomplished. Self-arsonist, feeling
the migraine begin, I throw it a desiccated branch,
watch it flame, taking comfort in the knowledge
that I have been labeled
phoenix. I will rise from all this ash.

-- *A.J. Huffman*

With Water

and forced palette of makeshift colors
I try to paint my life into plausibility.
A dash of spring to hold my eyes,
a slash of summer to breathe
life into my sallow skin.
I dart and dab, a sad attempt
at dabbling reality, but nothing holds.
One turn and shadows run
roughshot over the frame, forcing me to continue
to hang, a testimonial of a perfect mess.

-- A.J. Huffman

That is a Mineral Stain

my mother explained, pointing
to the strangely garish aqua streak
in the middle of the Cliffside.
The exquisite shade of disruption
against the muted earthy tones of the rock
reminded me of an abstract painting.
I smiled at the thought of this random
museum of nature, felt special for having been
allowed a moment of viewing, mourned its passing
as we continued on, speeding into the revived
redundancy of car climbing mountain's path.

-- A.J. Huffman

The Elements of Loss

Four light bulbs hung themselves in effigy.
They are ashamed of their part in the abuse
of the elements. The first died a slower death,
full of water. Its filament flooded with bubbles
of emotional release. The second died
in an instant, flared brighter for a moment
of complete consumption as if its glass body was
living flame. The third died peacefully,
recycled itself in burial, birthed anonymous
bud. The last died in absence. Suspended
in clarity, it breathed emptiness till the end,
dangled hollow as its gesture, an idol of apathetic air.

-- A.J. Huffman

from Sand this Coffin

I come to the water to wallow
in waves of regret. Emulating crab,
I crawl inside shell, wait for shadows
to pass. They linger longer than expected.
Panic becomes palpable. Shaking visibly,
I begin tunneling to tomorrow. *Deeper.*
Lone syllable vibrates through my body,
as arms become shovels, digging at almost
electrical pace. Soon I am silt soldier,
submerged. My eyes, alone, survive
to erase any print that could possibly be
construed as invitation, hesitation
or doubt.

-- A.J. Huffman

I Am Elemental

Four corners of the same circle,
I am daughter of the universe.
Transverse angel, I am tangible.
I breathe in atmosphere, expel
cosmic balance.

    I. I Am Earth

Composite minerals, I am trace
particles, bits of roots and reeds.
I am sedimentary, reflecting
pebbles of past. I am
passage, grounded prints
for eternity to follow

    II. I Am Air

Oxygen released, I am blue
skies and thickening fog. I am
breath, necessary life-giving intangibility.
I am invisible wind, embracing
skin, ruffling feathers. I am propulsion,
the force behind all aspects of flight.

    III. I Am Fire

Incendiary ignited, I am embodiment of warmth,
a burst of flame. Flint-made
figment of consumption. I am heated
furnace-filler. First gift,
stolen from the gods.

    IV. I Am Water

Cool condensation, I am pool,
puddle, river, lake, ocean. I am dripping

faucets and over-laden clouds.
I am thirst-quencher and fire-calmer.
I am more necessary than sustenance
for survival.

-- A.J. Huffman

Fire Drowns

a flint
a flare
a moment
        of flame
(ignition is temporary,
but exciting)
a flirtation
        with flotation
a deep breath
a plunge
        no splash, just
a trail
of smoke &
a sinking
of would-be
ash

                -- A.J. Huffman

Prelude to Death

He came to the beach to dig his own grave.
Tiny plastic shovel, a metaphor
for a desperate desire for youth, unattained.
Still he entered the cove as child, timid,
frightened of every shadow. Sitting cross-legged,
he dug with energy and enthusiasm, hollowed
the ground with ease, despite the inadequacy
of his equipment. He built a sandcastle
to act as headstone, to stand for fragility
of dreams. The tides would erase
this memory like so many others,
claim it as it would claim him: quickly,
quietly, and without remorse.

-- A.J. Huffman

I Am Fuse

No match can burn me.
Fire is already dripping
from my seams, ghosts
fueled by the perpetual heat
of anger. Frustration
is my name. I am waiting
for final ash to fall, trigger
the bomb I am destined
to become.

-- A.J. Huffman

Laundry Blows

from the back of a pick up
I can no longer recall us owning,
maybe a demo from the dealership
where my father worked in the parts
department. Ribbons of color fly
on residential streets, east
side, where it is not like anyone
would be grateful for the gifts.
It always happens after
they have been washed in my grandma's
machine, sometimes the ringer,
sometimes the automatic.
Dirty clothes clump together better,
shirts hold each other in their arms,
balls of underwear cling to the bottom
of the basket where socks roam,
free of their mates.
The Laundromat costs money and takes
devoted time, does not permit
multitasking, save a trash romance novel,
if we would stay quiet while my mom
reads, freckled legs crossed, crotch
of cut off denim shorts rubbing
in panty-less friction. Pants make the best
parachutes, sails catching wind, landing
in potholes to absorb the rest
of last night's summer rain.
Nothing could be funnier
to three pigtailed elementary school
girls riding in the bed, wishing for more
whites, flags to set free on highways.

-- April Salzano

The Only Way

for the man to pray is facing
south, and we are not a host
country, this woman, not
an Olympian. Yet, we are
on a boat, traveling to a place
where I will understand my son's
thoughts, and all my sins
will be forgiven if I can hold my breath
long enough to swim across the channel.
What one has to do
with the other, only dream can say.
Only dark so bright it has no choice
but to reveal will guide
the path of this wingless vessel through
the thickest of waters. At the edge
of the bed, an audience,
at the mouth of morning, an answer.

-- April Salzano

My Middle Name is Rain

Cloud of my pathetic fallacy falls
like nectar for self-imposed sadness.
I quench the thirst of every blade
of grass and knife alike. I martyr
myself for the cause of accumulation.
Dark, grey as April before the birth
of spring, showers that promise flowers,
but are no more magic than the sun.

-- April Salzano

My Middle Name is Water

I have not reached my freezing point.
I am moving under the surface. A skin
of ice cannot contain my current. I travel
in tributary to a destination larger.
I have been under every bridge
on my way home.

-- April Salzano

You Are at Home

among the trees, work boots and gloves,
tractors and chains.
One of your elms has died.
Its neighbor reached out
and caught hold as it collapsed. Together
they stayed, the living holding the dead,
no grudge, no resentment.
They would have remained
in that embrace, the green tree bearing burden
in silence without complaint,
but you intervened, upsetting the balance of things,
dropping the body in the wrong direction.
The ravine opened itself to swallow the remains, ready,
while the limbs of those still standing
waited in open embrace.

-- April Salzano

Tasting Air

At once thin, textureless membrane
of invisible barometric pressure,
and thick, humid moisture.
Empty oxygen, an opening that fills
spaces between here and there,
now and then, the breath
that separates tomorrow from today.
Every crevice, an occupied territory
in a war between molecules.

-- April Salzano

Smelling Smoke

on my breathe. Stale,
like celery. A reminder of resolutions
not kept. On the pillows.
In my hair.

in the air. Burning leaves.
Bodies singe in effigy
until a bottom layer, damp,
smolders and extinguishes effort.
Before rain mildews and snow
weighs us all,
shut-ins for another season.

in my house. A warning
preceding flames that may or may not
consume, claiming the irreplaceable.
Photos, flash drives,
documents, children.

in our bed. A slow effusion
wafting toward revolution
of fan blades. Dendritic tails separate,
thin. Exhaled, filtered
through lungs, travels faster.
Diffused like unkept promises.
The book we lost, Kama Sutra,
a wedding gift, an albatross
of positions not mastered.
Possibilities, ancient, ignored.

-- April Salzano

I Will Stop the Wind

from sighing
whispers of repression.
I will move the river to dry
bank of history,
ride the current
into tomorrow's shore.
I will follow memory's compass
out of borrowed time.

-- April Salzano

I Will Search the Soil

I will finger each wormhole,
pluck bugs from their dirty beds.
I will separate root from bulb,
flower from weed
to find new meaning in moss,
memory in mulch.
I will spend a lifetime
on hands and knees to leave
no stone unturned.

-- April Salzano

Author Bios

Sandra Anfang is a teacher, poet and visual artist. She is the author of four poetry collections and two chapbooks. Sandra has won several writing contests and awards, most recently, a first place award for her poem, "Surprise" in the 2014 Maggi Meyer Poetry Contest. Her poems have appeared in various journals including Poetalk, San Francisco Peace and Hope, West Trestle Review, Clementine Poetry Journal, The Tower Journal, Unbroken Literary Journal, Silver Birch Press, Porkbelly, Spillway 23, and The We' Moon Datebook 2016. Sandra has a chapbook, "Looking Glass Heart," due out from Finishing Line Press in January, 2016. She is the creator and host of the monthly poetry series, Rivertown Poets, in Petaluma, and a California Poet/Teacher in the schools. To write, for her, is to breathe.

Carol Alena Aronoff is a Ph.D., a psychologist, a teacher and a writer. Her poetry has been published in Comstock Review, Poetica, Sendero, Buckle&, Asphodel, Tiger 's Eye, Cyclamens & Swords, Quill & Parchment, Avocet, Bosque, 200 New Mexico Poems, Women Write Resistance, Before There is Nowhere to Stand, Malala: Poems for Malala Yousafzai, et al. She is a Pushcart Prize nominee, participated in Braided Lives, collaboration of artists/poets, Ekphrasis: Sacred Stories of the Southwest, and (A) Muses Poster Retrospective for the 2014 Taos Fall Arts Festival. The Nature of Music, was published by Blue Dolphin Publishing in 2005, Cornsilk in 2006, Her Soup Made the Moon Weep, in 2007, Blessings from an Unseen World in 2013 and Dreaming Earth's Body, in 2015. Currently, she resides in rural Hawaii--working her land, meditating in nature and writing.

Allen Ashley previously appeared in *A Touch of Saccharine* and *Life Is A Roller Coaster*. He writes regularly for the British Fantasy Society's "Journal" and "Newsletter". He works as a writing tutor in north London, UK, running five groups, including Clockhouse London Writers. His most recent books are, *Sensorama: Stories of the Senses,* as editor (Eibonvale Press, 2015) and *Dreaming Spheres: Poems of the Solar System* co-written with Sarah Doyle and published by PS Publishing (UK) in 2014. He has just finished guest-editing an issue of the online magazine *Sein und Werden* with the theme "The Restless Consumer."

Harvey J. Baine was born in the Mississippi Delta, spent his boyhood years in the Northeast, and as an adult, divided his years between North Florida and Northern Virginia before settling in Appomattox Virginia. He holds a BA from University of North Florida and an MFA in Creative Writing from American University. He has published poetry in journals such as; Big Muddy, REAL, HampdenSydney Poetry Review, Skidrow Penthouse, Cafe Review, The Cape Rock, and many others. As a student he concentrated on prose and published, (as his thesis) a collection of short stories entitled Cat Histories. (UMI) Currently, he works at Baine's Books and coffee, and spends most of his time at his desk, reading, and writing fiction.

Barbara Bald is a retired teacher, educational consultant and free-lance writer. Her poems have been published in a variety of anthologies: *The Other Side of Sorrow, The 2008 and 2010 Poets' Guide to New Hampshire, For Loving Precious Beast, Piscataqua Poems, The Widow's Handbook, Sun and Sand, In Gilded Frame* and other anthologies published by Kind of Hurricane Press. They have appeared in *The Northern New England Review, Avocet, Off the Coast* and in multiple issues of The Poetry Society of New Hampshire's publication: *The Poets' Touchstone*. Her work has been recognized in both national and local contests. Her recent full-length book is called *Drive-Through Window* and her new chapbook is entitled *Running on Empty*. Barb lives in Alton, NH with her cat Catcher and two Siamese Fighting fish.

James Bell was born in Scotland and now lives in France where he contributes photography and non-fiction to an English language journal. He has published two poetry collections: *the just vanished place* and *fishing for beginners*. He continues to publish poems online and on terra firma with recent appearances in *Long Exposure Magazine, The Journal, Tears In The Fence, Shearsman* and *Sarisvarti*.

Lana Bella has a diverse work of poetry and fiction anthologized, published and forthcoming with over one hundred journals, including a chapbook with Crisis Chronicles Press (early 2016), *Aurorean Poetry, Chiron Review, Contrary Magazine, QLSR* (Singapore), elsewhere, and Featured Artist with *Quail Bell Magazine*, among others. She divides her time between the US and the coastal town of Nha Trang, Vietnam, where she is a wife of a novelist, and a mom of two frolicsome imps.

Nancy Boutilier is the author of two poetry collections: *According to Her Contours* (Black Sparrow Press, 1992) and *On the Eighth Day Adam Slept Alone* (Black Sparrow Press, 2000), both finalists for the Lambda Literary Award in poetry. She currently teaches at Oberlin College.

Therese Broderick of Albany, New York, has been published in chapbooks, online, in anthologies, and in journals such as Spoon River Poetry Review and The Louisville Review. Among her awards are a nationally-competitive Overall Winner, a graduate school prize, a local Poet Laureate, and two First Places. She has served her local poetry community as a volunteer teacher, open mic hostess, contest judge, Board member, classroom guest, seminar panelist, and proud babysitter.

Tanya Bryan is a Canadian writer with work published in Latchkey Tales, Feathertale Review, and Longest Hours - thoughts while waiting anthology. She loves to travel, writing and drawing her experiences, which are often surreal and wonderful. She can be found @tanyabryan on Twitter.

Jane Burn is a North East based writer. She is a member of 52, the North East Women Writing Collective, the Black Light Writing Group and the Tees Women Poets. Her poems have been published in magazines such as Butcher's Dog, Ink Sweat & Tears, Nutshells and Nuggets, Alliterati, Lunar Poetry, The Stare's Nest, The Screech Owl, The Linnet's Wing, Obsessed With Pipework, Loch Raven Review, Deseeded Volume 3 and the Black Light Engine Room Literary Magazine. She was also day five on the New Boots and Pantisocracies project. Her work will also appear in Obsessed With Pipework and Zoomorphic and was long-listed for the Canterbury Poet of the Year Award, the National Poetry Competition and was commended in the Yorkmix 2014. Her work has been featured in Emma Press and Kind of a Hurricane Press Anthologies. She also had a single poem nominated for the Forward Prize.

Janet Rice Carnahan lives in La Jolla, California with her husband, Bruce, a retired physicist. Originally from Santa Cruz, California, Janet comes from a large family and has two adult children and one grandson. Her education, including a Master's degree, was in early childhood education, human development and family studies. Janet has been published in many online journals and in three anthologies. She also has one caption and a cover photo to her credit. Her other interests include traveling, walking on the beach, photography, metaphysics and healing work. Janet's web site, "Hear Earth Heart" explores some of these topics and offers her four self-published poetry books.

Alan Catlin has been publishing for decades now. Some days he feels like The Ancient of Days, other days, like The Old Man and the Sea. His latest anticipated collection of poetry is *Last Man Standing* from Lummox sometime in 2015.

Alexis Child hails from Toronto, Canada; horror in its purest form: a calculated crime both against the aspirations of the soul and affections of the heart. She worked at a Call Crisis Centre befriending demons of the mind that roam freely amongst her writings and lived with a Calico-cat child sleuthing all that went bump in the night & is haunted by the memory of her cat. She is once again signed to Nostilevo Records in the near future. Her goth rock band, Ceremony 7 will be re-issued on this record label in the Fall. *Her fiction has been featured in The House of Pain, Screams of Terror, SpecFicWorld.com, The Official Fields of the Nephilim Site, SinisterCity*, *and U.K.'s Dark Of Night Magazine.* Her poetry has been featured in numerous online and print publications, including *Aphelion, Black Petals, Blood Moon Rising, Estronomicon eZine, Death Head Grin, Midnight Lullabies Anthology, Sein und Werden, The Horror Zine and elsewhere.* Her first collection of poetry, "Devil in the Clock," will be released in print in the future by Witchfinder Press.

Joan Colby is a widely published, award-winning poet with 16 books to her credit. They include *Selected Poems, The Wingback Chair, Bittersweet, Ah Clio, Pro Forma* and others. Journals that include her work are *Poetry, Grand Street, Gargoyle, Atlanta Review, South Dakota Review, Hollins Critic* and others. She is the recipient of a Literary Fellowship from the Illinois Arts Council and has had many nominations to the Pushcart Press Prize and Best of the Net. Editor of a trade publication for over 30 years, she is associate editor of FutureCycle Press and Kentucky Review. She lives on a small horse-farm in northern Illinois.

Esteban Colon is an experiential educator and writer. His poetry has appeared in a variety of chap books, journals and anthologies and you can find his full length poetry collection Things I Learned the Hard Way on Amazon. He's a member of the Waiting 4 the Bus Poetry Collective and would love to see you sometime at an open mic in Chicago.

Craig Cornish is a New Hampshire native who has been writing poetry for 50 years but only in earnest for the last four years, after his retirement. He has been published multiple times to include the 2013 Kind of a Hurricane Press anthology *[Insert Coin Here]* and on contemporary artist Stephanie Deshpande's web site featuring a poem he wrote inspired by her painting "My Sleeping Child". He has only recently become active in seeking more publication.

Chella Courington is a writer and teacher. She's the author of three flash fiction chapbooks along with three chapbooks of poetry. Stories and poetry have appeared in numerous anthologies and journals including *SmokeLong, The Los Angeles Review, Nano Fiction,* and *The Collagist*. Her recent novella, *The Somewhat Sad Tale of the Pitcher and the Crow* (Pink.Girl.Ink.Press), is available at Amazon. Born and raised in the Appalachian south, she now lives in Santa Barbara, CA, with another writer and two cats.

Susan Dale has been published in *WestWard Quarterly, Ken *Again, Penman Review, Inner Art Journal, Garbanzo,* and *Linden Avenue.* In 2007, she won the grand prize for poetry from Oneswan. She has two published chapbooks on the internet: *Spaces Among Spaces* by languageandculture.org and *Bending the Spaces of Time* by *Barometric Pressure.*

Chip Dameron is the author of a travel book and seven collections of poetry, including two published this year: *Waiting for an Etcher* (Lamar University Press) and *Drinking from the River: New and Selected Poems, 1975-2015* (Wings Press). His poems and essays on contemporary writers have appeared in numerous journals and anthologies in the U.S. and abroad. A two-time nominee for the Pushcart Prize in poetry and a member of the Texas Institute of Letters, he lives and writes in Brownsville, Texas.

Theresa Darling has been published in *The Green Hills Literary Journal, Baily's Beads, Hellbender Journal, Kind of a Hurricane Press,* and *The Cellar Door*. Her poem "Another Departure" was nominated for the Pushcart Prize. She recently fulfilled a lifelong dream by moving to Vermont, where she hopes to live happily ever after with her husband Reg, and two shelter cats.

Brindley Hallam Dennis writes short fiction. He writes for reading aloud, and his stories have been performed by Liars Leagues in London, New York & Hong Kong. He lives in north Cumbria, within sight of three mountain tops and a sliver of Solway Firth. He blogs at www.Bhdandme.wordpress.com and can be found on Vimeo at BHDandMe. His books are available on Amazon.

Evelyn Deshane has appeared in Plenitude Magazine, The Rusty Toque, and is forthcoming in Tesseracts 19: Superhero Universe. Their chapbook, Mythology, was released in 2015 with The Steel Chisel. Evelyn (pron. Eve-a-lyn) received an MA from Trent University and currently studying for PhD at Waterloo University. Visit them at: evedeshane.wordpress.com

Eric Dodson has appeared in many New Zealand literary magazines including *Takahe* and *Poetry NZ*. He is retired and lives in sunny Tauranga Bay Of Plenty, New Zealand.

Karen Douglass is a Colorado writer who has published short fiction, poems and five books of poetry. She has a BS (Chapman College), an MA (Georgia Southern) and an MFA (Vermont College). She is a co-host for an ongoing poetry reading in Lafayette CO, a member of Lighthouse Writers' Workshop, Colorado Independent Publishers Association (board member), and Boulder Writers' Workshop. Her latest book is a novel, *Accidental Child*. You can find her publication list at www.KVDbooks.com.

morgan downie writes short stories and poetry. He has been anthologised widely, and appeared on shortlists from the Macallan and Orange short fiction prizes to the Bridport poetry prize. His first collection *stone and sea* was published by Calder Wood press. This was followed by *distances*, a photopoetry collection in English and Romanian, and *a lazarus*, a chapbook length collection that was shortlisted for the qartsilunni prize.

Inna Dulchevsky spent her early school years in Belarus. She currently resides in Brooklyn, New York. She was awarded the First Prize 2014 David B. Silver Poetry Competition. Inna's work has been published in numerous anthologies, books, and journals including *Pyrokinection, Jellyfish Whispers, Petals in the Pan Anthology,* book *Lavende*r, *The Cannon's Mouth,The Otter, New Poetry, Calliope Magazine, Aquillrelle Anthology,* 4th annual *LUMMOX Poetry Anthology, Antheon, KNOT Magazine, and Calliope Magazine Anniversary Issue.* Her interests include metaphysics, philosophy, meditation and yoga. The light and expansion of consciousness through the connection with inner-self and nature are essential in the writing of her poetry.

J.K. Durick is a writing teacher at the Community College of Vermont and an online writing tutor. His recent poems have appeared in *Camel Saloon*, *Black Mirror*, *Poetry Pacific*, *Eye on life Magazine*, and *Leaves of Ink*.

Lucia Galloway has published two poetry collections: *Venus and Other Losses* (Plain View) and *Playing Outside* (Finishing Line). Recent work appears or is forthcoming in *Tar River Poetry, Comstock Review, Midwest Quarterly, Inlandia, Mason's Road,* and *Poemeleon*; and the anthologies *Thirty Days* (Tupelo) and *Wide Awake: Poets of Los Angeles and Beyond* (Beyond Baroque). A top-prize winner in Rhyme Zone's 2014-15 Poetry Contest for her poem "Open to the Elements." Galloway also won the Quills Edge inaugural poetry chapbook competition for *The Garlic Peelers*. Her manuscripts have been finalists for Tupelo's Snowbound Chapbook award and the Able Muse Book Prize. She hosts *Fourth Sundays*, a reading series in Claremont, California.

Brigitte Goetze is a biologist, goat farmer, writer, and lives near Oregon's Coast Range. Her most recent poems can be found in *Agave Literary Journal* and *Mused*. Her web address is: brigittegoetzewriter.weebly.com.

Joan Goodreau has published two recent books: her memoir *Strangers Together: How My Son's Autism Changed My Life* and her poetry book *Another Secret Shared*. Two of her plays about breast cancer have been produced this year.

Rick Hartwell is a retired middle school teacher (remember the hormonally-challenged?) living in Southern California. He believes in the succinct, that the small becomes large; and, like the Transcendentalists and William Blake, that the instant contains eternity. Given his "druthers," if he's not writing, Rick would rather still be tailing plywood in a mill in Oregon. He can be reached at rdhartwell@gmail.com.

H. Edgar Hix writes in Minneapolis, Minnesota, U.S.A., a place of many elemental features, most predominately water. He is originally from Oklahoma, a place of wind and lightning.

Ruth Holzer has appeared in previous Kind of a Hurricane anthologies, as well as in a variety of journals including California Quarterly, THEMA, Southern Poetry Review and RHINO. She has published three chapbooks, most recently "A Woman Passing" (Green Fuse Press).

Liz Hufford is a practitioner of feng shui, harmonizing the elements of wood, fire, earth, metal, and water within and without the home. She is the published author of poems, flash fiction, articles, essays, and short stories.

W. Luther Jett is a native of Montgomery County, Maryland, and has recently completed his first novel. He began writing shortly after learning how to hold a crayon and started transcribing his ideas onto paper shortly thereafter. His poetry has been published in numerous journals, including: The GW Review, Poetica, Syncopated City, Synæsthesia, ABRAXAS, Scribble, Beltway, Innisfree, Xanadu, Haiku Journal, Steam Ticket, Potomac Review, and Main Street Rag. Luther appeared with the Cabaradio troupe during the 2006 Capital Fringe Festival. His poetry performance piece, Flying to America, debuted at the 2009 Capital Fringe Festival. He was a featured reader during the Summer 2009 Joaquin Miller Cabin Series, and during the Kensington Row Bookshop 2010 series. His poem, "The Chalk House" took first place in the Jean Stainback Schmidt Poetry Contest sponsored by the Long Island Poetry Collective; he was also a winner in the Moving Words Poetry Competition for 2011, sponsored by the Arlington County (VA) Arts Program. He was named a semi-finalist in the 2014 WordWorks Washington Prize competition. His chapbook, "Not Quite" was recently released by Finishing Line Press.

Michael Lee Johnson lived ten years in Canada during the Vietnam era. He is a Canadian and USA citizen. Today he is a poet, freelance writer, amateur photographer, small business owner in Itasca, Illinois. He has been published in more than 880 small press magazines in 27 countries, and he edits 10 poetry sites. Author's website http://poetryman.mysite.com/. Michael is the author of *The Lost American: From Exile to*

Freedom (136 page book) ISBN: 978-0-595-46091-5, several chapbooks of poetry, including *From Which Place the Morning Rises* and *Challenge of Night and Day, and Chicago Poems.* He also has over 77 poetry videos on YouTube as of 2015: https://www.youtube.com/user/poetrymanusa/videos

Lori Kiefer teaches creative writing to adults in a mental health day centre and provides counselling support to students at a London University. She is working towards a first collection and also enjoys writing haiku poetry. Her poems are published in several anthologies and she has written several pantomimes.

Noel King was born and lives in Tralee, Co Kerry. In this his 50th year, he has reached his 1000th publication of a poem, haiku or short story in magazines and journals in thirty-eight countries. His poetry collections are published by Salmon: *Prophesying the Past,* (2010), *The Stern Wave* (2013) and *Sons* (2015). He has edited more than fifty books of work by others and was poetry editor of *Revival Literary Journal* (Limerick Writers' Centre) in 2012/13. Anthology publications include *The Second Genesis: An Anthology of Contemporary World Poetry* (AR.A.W.,India, 2014).

Steve Klepetar has appeared in nine countries, in such journals as *Boston Literary Magazine, Deep Water, Antiphon, Red River Review, Snakeskin, Ygdrasil,* and many others. Several of his poems have been nominated for the Pushcart Prize and Best of the Net. Recent collections include *Speaking to the Field Mice* (Sweatshoppe Publications, 2013), *My Son Writes a Report on the Warsaw Ghetto* (Flutter Press, 2013) and *Return of the Bride of Frankenstein* (Kind of a Hurricane Press).

Andrea Lewis writes short stories, flash fiction, and essays from her home on Vashon Island, Washington. Her work has appeared in many literary journals, including Prairie Schooner, Catamaran Literary Reader, and Cutthroat. Two of her stories have been nominated for the Pushcart Prize. She is a founding member of Richard Hugo House, a place for writers in Seattle. More of her work can be seen at www.andrealewis.org.

Lyn Lifshin has published over 130 books and chapbooks including 3 from Black Sparrow Press: *Cold Comfort, Before It's Light* and *Another Woman Who Looks Like Me.* Before *Secretariat: The Red Freak, The Miracle,* Lifshin published her prize winning book about the short lived beautiful race horse Ruffian, *The Licorice Daughter: My Year With Ruffian* and *Barbaro: Beyond Brokenness.* Recent books include *Ballroom, All the Poets Who Have Touched Me, Living and Dead. All True, Especially The Lies, Light At the End: The Jesus Poems, Katrina, Mirrors, Persphone, Lost In The Fog, Knife Edge* & *Absinthe: The Tango Poems.* NYQ books published *A Girl Goes into The Woods.* Also just out: *For the Roses* poems after Joni Mitchell and *Hitchcock Hotel* from Danse Macabre. *Secretariat: The Red Freak, The Miracle.* And *Tangled as the Alphabet,-- The Istanbul Poems from* NightBallet Press Just released as well *Malala,* the dvd of *Lyn Lifshin: Not Made of Glass. The Marilyn Poems* was just released from Rubber Boots Press. An update to her Gale Research Autobiography is out: *Lips, Blues, Blue Lace: On The Outside.* Also just out is a dvd of the documentary film about her: *Lyn Lifshin: Not Made Of Glass.* Just out: Femme Eterna and *Moving Through Stained Glass: the Maple Poems.* Forthcoming: *Degas Little Dancer* and *The Silk Road.* Her web: www.lynlifshin.com

Jack e Lorts is a retired educator living in a small, isolated town in Eastern Oregon and has appeared extensively, if infrequently, over the past 40+ years in such magazines as *Arizona Quarterly, Kansas Quarterly, English Journal, Agnostic Lobster, Fishtrap, Oregon English Journal, Oregon East* and *High Desert Journal,* among others. Author of three chapbooks, *The Daughter Poems & Others...* and *The Meeting-Place of Words,* published by Pudding House, and *Dear Gilbert Sorrentino & Other Poems* from Finishing Line Press. He has also assembled several "serial poems" (collaborative poems by up to 20 different poets) which have seen magazine and/or book publication by Talent House Press, Wordcraft of Oregon and Traprock Books. Active in local and state Democratic politics, the past six years he served as Mayor of Fossil, Oregon.

Hillary Lyon is founder of and editor for the small poetry publishing house, Subsynchronous Press. Her work has appeared in *EOAGH, Shadow Train, Eternal Haunted Summer, Red River Review, Red Fez*, and *Shot Glass Journal*, among others. She lives in southern Arizona.

Jennifer MacBain-Stephens went to NYU's Tisch School of the Arts and currently lives in the DC area with her family. She is the author of six chapbooks. Recent ones are forthcoming from *Dancing Girl Press*, *Crisis Chronicles Press* and *Shirt Pocket Press*. Her first full length poetry collection is forthcoming from *Lucky Bastard Press*. Recent work can be seen / is forthcoming at, *Pretty Owl Poetry*, *Yes, Poetry*, *Gargoyle*, *Jet Fuel Review*, *glitterMOB*, *Pith*, *So to Speak*, *Apple Valley Review*, *Otis Nebula*, *Freezeray*, *Entropy*, *Right Hand Pointing*, and *decomP*. For more, visit: http://jennifermacbainstephens.wordpress.com/.

Don Mager has published several chapbooks and volumes of poetry: *To Track the Wounded One, Glosses, That Which is Owed to Death, Borderings, Good Turns* and *The Elegance of the Ungraspable, Birth Daybook Drive Time* and Russian Riffs. He is retired with degrees from Drake University (BA), Syracuse University (MA) and Wayne State University (PhD). He was the Mott University Professor of English at Johnson C. Smith University from 1998-2004 where he served as Dean of the College of Arts and Letters (2005-2011). As well as a number of scholarly articles, he has published over 200 poems and translations from German, Czech and Russian. He lives in Charlotte, NC. *Us Four Plus Four* is an anthology of translations from eight major Soviet-era Russian poets. It is unique because it tracks almost a half century of their careers by simply placing the poems each wrote to the others in chronological order. The 85 poems represent one of the most fascinating conversations in poems produced by any group of poets in any language or time period. From poems and infatuation and admiration to anger and grief and finally to deep tribute, this anthology invites readers into the unfolding lives of such inimitable creative forces as Anna Akhmatova, Boris Pasternak, Marina Tsvetaeva and Osip Mandelstam.

Susan Mahan has been writing poetry since her husband died in 1997. She has written 350 poems and gotten many of them published.

Kim Malinowski received her B.A. at West Virginia University and her M.F.A. from American University. She is currently an Advanced Poetry student at The Writers Studio. Her work has appeared in *Mythic Delirium, Mad Poets Review, Souvenir, War, Literature, and the Arts,* and others.

Amanda M. May attained her Master's Degree in Language and Literature from Central Michigan University in 2012. After teaching English for two years in Japan, she returned to America for the next adventure and relocated to Florida in 2015 for work. Her flash fiction appeared in former Kind of a Hurricane Press anthologies, and her poetry, short stories, and essays have been published by various literary magazines. She is currently editing her first novel, her seventh National Novel Writing Month victory, with more seriousness than her former manuscripts.

Joan McNerney has been included in numerous literary magazines such as *Camel Saloon, Seven Circle Press, Dinner with the Muse, Blueline, Missing of the Birds,* and included in Bright Hills Press, Kind of A Hurricane Press and Poppy Road Review anthologies. She has been nominated three times for Best of the Net.

Mark J. Mitchell studied writing at UC Santa Cruz under Raymond Carver, George Hitchcock and Barbara Hull. His work has appeared in various periodicals over the last thirty five years, as well as the anthologies *Good Poems, American Places, Hunger Enough, Retail Woes* and *Line Drives.*. It has also been nominated for both Pushcart Prizes and The Best of the Net. Two full length collections are in the works: *Lent 1999* is coming soon from Leaf Garden Press and *This Twilight World* will be published by Popcorn Press. His chapbook, *Three*

Visitors has recently been published by Negative Capability Press. *Artifacts and Relics*, another chapbook was just released by Folded Word and his novel, *Knight Prisoner,* was recently published by Vagabondage Press and a another novel, *A Book of Lost Songs* is coming soon from Wild Child Publishing. He lives in San Francisco with his wife, the documentarian and filmmaker Joan Juster.

Ralph Monday is Associate Professor of English at Roane State Community College in Harriman, TN, and published in over 50 journals. A chapbook, All American Girl and Other Poems, was published in July 2014. A book Lost Houses and American Renditions was published May 2015 by Aldrich Press.

George Moore has a new poetry collection, *Saint Agnes Outside the Walls* set to be published with FutureCycle Press in 2016. His other collections include *Children's Drawings of the Universe* (Salmon Poetry 2015) and *The Hermits of Dingle* (FutureCycle 2013). Poems have appeared in *The Atlantic, North American Review, Poetry*, and *Colorado Review*. He has recently moved from Colorado to the south shore of Nova Scotia.

Heidi Morrell lives and writes in Los Angeles, is married and lives in an old house with her two kids, & patient husband. Heidi's work has appeared in magazines, anthologies, among many: East Coast literary Review; Hurricane Press; Emerge Literary Journal; Poetry Pacific; Rotary Dial, Canadian; Outside In Lit Magazine; Mothers Always Write; Tomato Slices; Young Ravens Lit Review; Plum Tree Tavern - Fiction: Blue Skirt Press; Oval Magazine, Ink Monkey Press; Dual Coast Magazine, and a poetry *Chapbook* from Finishing Line Press.

Kacper Niburski doesn't want you to think he has made it, even though he's made it here and here has it made. Better than there where he currently is: clawing through a Master's degree like an amateur and hiding creeping baldness with hats. Find his work http://kacperniburski.wordpress.com

Suzanne O'Connell lives in Los Angeles where she is a poet and a clinical social worker. Her work can be found in *Forge, Atlanta Review, Crack The Spine, Lummox Journal, Blue Lake Review, G.W.*

Review, Reed Magazine, Permafrost, Mas Tequila Review, The Round, The Griffin, Sanskrit, Foliate Oak, Talking River, Organs of Vision and Speech Literary Magazine, Willow Review, The Tower Journal, Poetry Super Highway, Thin Air Magazine, Fre&d, The Manhattanville Review, poeticdiversity, The Evansville Review, Serving House Journal, Silver Birch Press, Schuylkill Valley Journal, and *Licking River Review.* She was a recipient of Willow Review's annual award for 2014 for the poem "Purple Summers." She is a member of Jack Grapes' L.A. Poets and Writers Collective. suzanneoconnell-poet.com

Mary C. O'Malley is a poet and playwright. She has both a MSW and MFA and lives in the greater Cleveland , Ohio area.

Carl Palmer of Old Mill Road in Ridgeway VA now lives in University Place WA. He has a 2015 contest winning poem riding buses somewhere in Seattle. Carl is a Pushcart Prize and Micro Award nominee. MOTTO: Long Weekends Forever www.authorsden.com/carlpalmer

Simon Perchik is an attorney whose poems have appeared in *Partisan Review, The Nation, Osiris, Poetry, The New Yorker*, and elsewhere. His most recent collection is *Almost Rain,* published by River Otter Press (2013). For more information, free e-books and his essay titled "Magic, Illusion and Other Realities" please visit his website at www.simonperchik.com.

Richard King Perkins II is a state-sponsored advocate for residents in long-term care facilities. He lives in Crystal Lake, IL with his wife Vickie and daughter Sage. He is a three-time Pushcart nominee and a Best of the Net nominee whose work has appeared in hundreds of publications including The Louisiana Review, Bluestem, Emrys Journal, Sierra Nevada Review, Roanoke Review, The Red Cedar Review and The William and Mary Review. He has poems forthcoming in Sobotka Literary Magazine, The Alembic, Old Red Kimono and Milkfist. He was a recent finalist in The Rash Awards, Sharkpack Alchemy, Writer's Digest and Bacopa Literary Review poetry contests.

Freya Pickard is a cancer survivor, trying to re-discover her creativity after bowel cancer, surgery and chemotherapy. She is the author of Dragonscale Leggings and is currently writing poetry in order to try and get her creative flow to return. Freya blogs at either http://purehaiku.wordpress.com or http://dragonscaleclippings.wordpress.com depending on how she is feeling.

Tim Roberts is a flash-fictioneer with a creative sweet-spot between 8 and 9 a.m. His work has won several prizes and been published by the Faber Academy, Paper Swans Press and appears in The 2015 National Flash Fiction Day Anthology.

Francesca Sasnaitis is a Melbourne-based writer and artist, currently embarked on a PhD in Creative Writing at the University of Western Australia. Her poetry, fiction and reviews have most recently appeared in *Australian Book Review*, *Cordite*, *Southerly*, *Sydney Review of Books*, *The Trouble with Flying and other stories* and *Westerly*.

Emily Jo Scalzo has an MFA in Fiction from California State University, Fresno. She currently resides in Muncie, Indiana, and is an assistant professor at Ball State University. Her work has been published in *Mobius: The Journal of Social Change, The Mindful Word, Ms. Fit Magazine,* and *Third Wednesday.*

Keenan Schott is a poet, musician, and grocery clerk from St. Louis, Missouri. His work has been published in *The Camel Saloon, Rasasvada,* and *The (Truman) Monitor.* His band Bong Threat, for which he writes the lyrics and a simple majority of the music, has been reviewed on The Sludgelord and can be heard on Bandcamp, Spotify, and various other streaming websites and digital download stores. Although Keenan works within various genres and mediums, across the board his art deals primarily with finding purpose in a meaningless, absurd reality by means of a loving community.

Belinda Singleton has had a varied career in Communications, including 12 years as a Director of the English Speaking Board (International) Ltd and a similar length as Chief Assessor for London and the South-East for all Communications schemes for City & Guilds of London Institute. She returned to writing poetry at the end of 2007. She has been published in various respected poetry magazines in the UK. and has been a prizewinner in open poetry competitions, including winning the John Clare Prize in 2011. She reads at London poetry venues and is Chairman of the long-standing Wey Poets group, based in Guildford, Surrey.

J. J. Steinfeld is a Canadian fiction writer, poet, and playwright who lives on Prince Edward Island, where he is patiently waiting for Godot's arrival and a phone call from Kafka. While waiting, he has published sixteen books, including *Disturbing Identities* (Stories, Ekstasis Editions), *Should the Word Hell Be Capitalized?* (Stories, Gaspereau Press), *Would You Hide Me?* (Stories, Gaspereau Press), *An Affection for Precipices* (Poetry, Serengeti Press),*Misshapenness* (Poetry, Ekstasis Editions), *A Glass Shard and Memory* (Stories, Recliner Books), *Identity Dreams and Memory Sounds* (Poetry, Ekstasis Editions), and *Madhouses in Heaven, Castles in Hell* (Stories, Ekstasis Editions). His short stories and poems have appeared in numerous anthologies and periodicals internationally, and over forty of his one-act plays and a handful of full-length plays have been performed in Canada and the United States. http://www.ekstasiseditions.com/recenthtml/madhouses.htm

Emily Strauss has an M.A. in English, but is self-taught in poetry, which she has written since college Over 250 of her poems appear in a wide variety of online venues and in anthologies, in the U.S. and abroad. The natural world is generally her framework; she also considers the stories of people and places around her and personal histories. She is a semi-retired teacher living in California.

Linda Strever had a poetry collection,*Against My Dreams*, released in 2013 and her novel, *Don't Look Away*, in 2015. Her poetry has been published in numerous journals and anthologies. Winner of the Lois Cranston Memorial Poetry Prize, her work has been a finalist for the New Issues Poetry Prize, the Levis

Poetry Prize and the Ohio State University Press Award in Poetry, as well as the Eludia Award in fiction from Hidden River Arts. A Pushcart Prize nominee, she has an MFA from Brooklyn College and lives in Olympia, Washington.

Marianne Szlyk is a professor at Montgomery College and the editor of The Song Is... Recently, she published her second chapbook, I Dream of Empathy, with Flutter Press. Her first (Listening to Electric Cambodia, Looking Up at Trees of Heaven) was published by Kind of a Hurricane Press. Her poems have appeared in Long Exposure, ken*again, Of/with, bird's thumb, Solar Nation, Snapping Twig, Silver Birch Press' Where I Live Series, Jellyfish Whispers, Napalm and Novocain, Poppy Road Review, and other online and print venues including Kind of a Hurricane Press' anthologies. She thanks her friend, the Boston artist Tamara Safford for introducing her to the haunting work of Roni Horn.

Barbara Tate is an award winning artist and writer. She was recently awarded 2nd place in United Haiku and Tanka Society's Samurai Haibun Competition, won 1st place in Gulf Coast Writers Assoc., annual competition in the Poetry Category, was a finalist in the Poetry Society of Tennessee NE competition and a finalist in the United Poet Laureate International competition for the Alexander Fui Sak Chang Award--short free verse in Chinese or English. Her work has appeared in *Modern Haiku, Contemporary Haibun Online, Frogpond, Cattails, Bear Creek Haiku, Storyteller Magazine* and *Switch (the Difference)* Anthology, among others. She is a member of the Haiku Society of America, Gulf Coast Writers Assoc., and the United Haiku & Tanka Society. She currently resides in Winchester, TN.

Peter Taylor has published *Trainer*, *The Masons,* and *Aphorisms.* His poems have been published internationally in *Anansesem, Aperçus Quarterly, Call & Response, Contemporary Verse 2, Construction, The Copperfield Review, Descant, Eunoia, Fade, Frostwriting, The Glass Coin, Grain, Ink, Sweat & Tears, The Linnet's Wings, Nether, Petrichor Review, Phantom Kangaroo, Pirene's Fountain, Poetry Australia, Pyrta, and Step Away Magazine.* His experimental verse play, *Antietam,* won honorable mention in Winning Writer's War

Poetry Contest in Northampton, Massachusetts. He lives in Aurora, Canada.

Sarah Thursday calls Long Beach, California, her home, where she advocates for local poets and poetry events. She runs a poetry website called CadenceCollective.net, co-hosts a monthly reading with G. Murray Thomas, and founded Sadie Girl Press. Her first full-length poetry collection, *All the Tiny Anchors*, is available now. Find and follow her to learn more on SarahThursday.com, Facebook, or Twitter.

Jari Thymian has appeared in publications including *tinywords, The Pedestal, FRiGG, The Furious Gazelle, The Journal of Compressed Creative Arts, and American Tanka*. Her poetry has been nominated for Best of the Net and a Pushcart Prize. She volunteers year-round in state and national parks in the USA.

Dennis Trujillo is a former soldier and middle/high school math teacher who happens to love poetry. Most recent selections are forthcoming or already published with *Atlanta Review, Ascent, Agave, THEMA, Slant, 3Elements Review, Your Daily Poem, Wild Goose Poetry Review, Silver Birch Press*, and *Snapdragon: A Journal of Art and Healing*. He runs and does yoga each morning for grounding, focus, and for the sheer joy of it.

Susan Vespoli lives in Phoenix with her 3-legged dog Jack. She is a teacher, poet, and born-again-bicyclist. Susan received her MFA from Antioch University L.A. and has had poems and essays published in various online and print journals.

Claire Walker lives in Worcestershire, UK. Her poetry has appeared in various print and online magazines including The Interpreter's House, Ink Sweat and Tears, And Other Poems, Snakeskin and Emerge Literary Journal. In June 2014 she was runner up in the 2014/2015 Worcestershire Poet Laureate Competition.

Loretta Diane Walker is a multiple Pushcart nominee. She has published two collections of poetry and her manuscript In This House is forth coming in 2015. Loretta was recently named "Statesman in the Arts" by the Heritage Council of Odessa. Walker's work has appeared in numerous publications, most recently *Her Texas, Texas Poetry Calendar 2015, Pushing Out the Boat International Journal, San Pedro River Review, Illya's Honey, Red River Review, Diversity: Austin International Poetry Festival, Boundless Poetry: Rio Grande Valley International Poetry Festival, Pushing the Envelope: Epistolary Poems, Perception Literary Magazine,* and is forthcoming in *Connecticut River Review, The Texas Poetry Calendar 2016,* and *Siblings: Our First Macrocosm.* Her manuscript Word Ghetto won the 2011 Bluelight Press Book Award. She teaches music in Odessa, Texas. Loretta received a BME from Texas Tech University and earned a MA from The University of Texas of the Permian Basin.

Connie K Walle is a life-long resident of Tacoma, Washington, is President and founder of Puget Sound Poetry Connection where she hosts the "Distinguished Writer Series" now in its 25rd year. Connie founded *Our Own Words*, a teen writing contest now in its 19th year. Her awards include: 1998 Margaret K Williams Award in support of the arts; Washington Poets Association Faith Beamer Cooks Award. She is a mother of three, grandmother of seven and currently retired. A few of her publications *include Floating Bridge Press, Raven Chronicle, Tahoma's Shadow,* and *Cradle Song* and Kind of a Hurricane Press.

Mercedes Webb-Pullman graduated from IIML Victoria University Wellington with MA in Creative Writing in 2011. Her poems and the odd short story have appeared online, in print and in her books *Food 4 Thought, Numeralla Dreaming, After the Danse, Ono, Looking for Kerouac, Tasseography, Bravo Charlie Foxtrot* and *Collected poems 2008 - 2014.* She lives on the Kapiti Coast, New Zealand. www.benchpress.co.nz

J.R. West is 30 years old, born and raised in rural Maine. Since graduating with an English degree and running the University of Utah's undergraduate literary journal Enormous Rooms, he's been employed as a technical writer for an infamous electronics company in Silicon Valley. His literary influences range from naturalism to surrealism, existentialists, beat poets—especially Gary Snyder, and for good measure Yeats and Rumi. They're all fighting it out upstairs. When he's not traveling for outdoor pursuits, he's writing poetry, technobabble, or chewing over the next great fantasy novel. He also loves to collaborate with other writers on comedy skits, screenplays, and writes the odd commissioned article. His most recent publication was by Everyday Poems for his poem "The Buoy at St. Margaret's Hope."

Mary L. Westcott has been writing poetry for more than 25 years. She received an MA in Writing from Johns Hopkins University in 2010. She has been published in more than 55 literary journals. She has published 6 books of poetry, including the latest from Balboa Press, called *Fluttering on Earth*, a poetic memoir. She retired from the National Institutes of Health, and lives in Central Florida.

Shannon Connor Winward is a poetry editor for Devilfish Review and a staff writer for Pop Culture Madness. Her writing has appeared or is forthcoming in *Pedestal Magazine, Gargoyle, Strange Horizons, Literary Mama, Hip Mama,* and *Star*Line,* to name a few. Shannon placed as a semi-finalist in the Writers of the Future Contest, and as runner-up for the Emerging Artist Fellowship in Literature with the Delaware Division of the Arts in both 2014 and 2015. Her poetry collection, Undoing Winter (Finishing Line Press) was nominated for an Elgin Award. Visit Shannon on the web at www.shannonconnorwinward.com.

Diana Woodcock won the 2010 Venice Quebodeaux International Poetry Prize for Women with her first full-length collection, *Swaying on the Elephant's Shoulders*. Her six chapbooks include *Beggar in the Everglades, Desert Ecology: Lessons and Visions, Tamed by the Desert, In the Shade of the Sidra Tree, Mandala,* and *Travels of a Gwai Lo.* Widely published in literary journals, her poems have been nominated for the Pushcart Prize and Best of the Net Award. Since receiving an M.F.A. degree in Creative Writing in 2004, she has been teaching writing courses at Virginia Commonwealth University in Qatar/School of the Arts. Previously, she spent nearly eight years working in Tibet, Macau, and on the Thai-Cambodian border. She is a PhD candidate (creative writing/poetry) at Lancaster University.

Kirby Wright films his first short in Hollywood this September. He is trapped between joy and terror.

Xanadu lives in *Iv*, Space of Infinite Imagination, Public's Home 0. It consists in publications, performances and exhibits in poetry and art contexts.

Mantz Yorke lives in Manchester, England. His poems have appeared in *Butcher's Dog*, *Lunar Poetry*, *Prole*, *Revival* and *The Brain of Forgetting* magazines, in e-magazines and in anthologies in the UK and US. He has contributed to various poetry gatherings in the north of England.

Changming Yuan is an 8-time Pushcart nominee, grew up in rural China, started to learn English at 19 and published several monographs on translation before moving to Canada. Currently co-editing *Poetry Pacific* with Allen Qing Yuan in Vancouver, Yuan has poetry appearing in 1009 literary publications across 31 countries, including *Best Canadian Poetry, BestNewPoemsOnline,* and *Threepenny Review.*

About The Editors

A.J. Huffman has published eleven solo chapbooks and one joint chapbook through various small presses. Her new poetry collection, *Another Blood Jet,* is now available from Eldritch Press. She has three more poetry collections forthcoming: *A Few Bullets Short of Home* from mgv2>publishing, *Degeneration* from Pink Girl Ink, and *A Bizarre Burning of Bees* from Transcendent Zero Press. She is a Multiple Pushcart Prize nominee, and has published over 2100 poems in various national and international journals, including *Labletter, The James Dickey Review, Bone Orchard, EgoPHobia,* and *Kritya*. She is also the founding editor of Kind of a Hurricane Press. www.kindofahurricanepress.com

April Salzano is the co-editor at Kind of a Hurricane Press and is currently working on a memoir about raising a child with autism, as well as several collections of poetry. Her work has been twice nominated for a Pushcart Award and has appeared in journals such as *The Camel Saloon, Centrifugal Eye, Deadsnakes, Visceral Uterus, Salome, Poetry Quarterly, Writing Tomorrow* and *Rattle*. Her chapbook, *The Girl of My Dreams,* is available from Dancing Girl Press. Her poetry collection, *Future Perfect,* is forthcoming from Pink Girl Ink. More of her work can be read at aprilsalzano.blogspot.com

Printed in Great Britain
by Amazon